ZEN

IN THE AMERICAN GRAIN

ZEN
IN
THE
AMERICAN
GRAIN

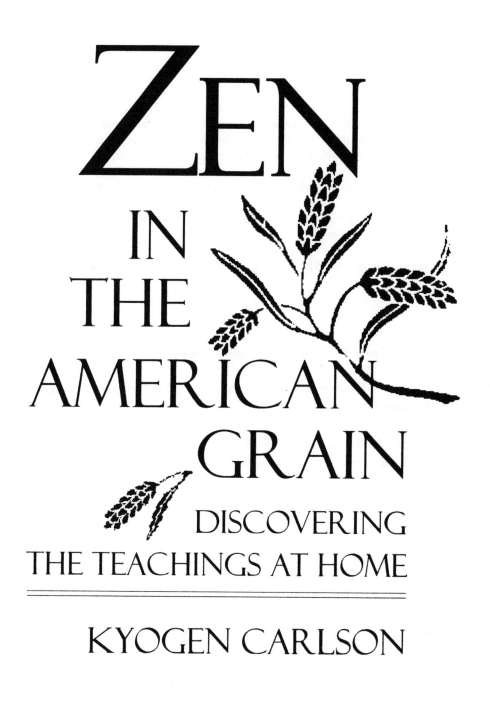

DISCOVERING
THE TEACHINGS AT HOME

KYOGEN CARLSON

STATION HILL

Published by Station Hill Press, Inc., Barrytown, New York 12507.

Distributed by the Talman Company, 131 Spring Street, Suite 201 E-N, New York, New York 10012.

Cover and book design by Susan Quasha, assisted by Dominick Amarante and Vicki Hickman.

Library of Congress Cataloging-in-Publication Data
Carlson, Kyogen.
    Zen in the american grain : discovering the teachings at home / Kyogen Carlson.
       p. cm.
    ISBN 0-88268-158-3 : $9.95
    1. Spiritual life — Zen Buddhism. I. Title
BQ9288.C37 1994
294.3'927 — dc20   94-39656
                                                    CIP

Manufactured in the United States of America

This book is dedicated to the members of Dharma Rain Zen Center. The need to meet your sincere desire for the Dharma in an appropriate way is what has propelled Gyokuko and me forward in new and wonderful ways in our own efforts in practice.

Readers of this small volume will notice that nowhere in the text do I mention my own teacher by name, nor do I name the monastery where Gyokuko and I trained. This is to comply with our teacher's request not to link our names with hers, except in basic biographical information. She also wishes me to state that we do not represent her, nor the monastery in any official way. Her reasons are her own, and I merely honor her request. Yet I must acknowledge that any merit in this book comes through the lineage tradition of practice, and its shortcomings are entirely my own.

GKC

PREFACE

"Zen" is now an American word. It's not well-defined yet, perhaps, but in common usage it denotes being "in sync" with something; a state of harmony between subject and object. It also smacks of flaky California New Age Gurus. Still, the basic implication is not half bad. When you dig a little further into the American Buddhist scene, however, you find that even among Buddhists, Zen has a mixed image. Some see in it militaristic discipline and orderliness to the point of obsession, while to others it is a tradition of iconoclasts, with leanings toward spontaneity and the artistic. Some even see it as a license to do whatever they want, thinking that is what zen spontaneity means. As it is developing in America, Zen does include a little of all these things, for better or worse. For me, at the heart of it, Zen is about experiencing the wonder and mystery that fills ordinary, mundane existence but is usually hidden from our sight. Zen practice points to a deep awareness of the here and now, and in this it bears some resemblance to the common usage of the word "zen." But although this awareness sounds great to many people, when it gets right down to it, they often don't want it to include the boring, vexing, irritating aspects of daily life. The fact is, many people seeking solace in spiritual practices such as Zen are running from themselves. In that regard, they aren't much different from the pleasure-seekers so common in our culture, frenetically chasing one diversion after another. To begin Zen practice seriously requires an end to this evasion of self. It begins with raising and recognizing "the mind that seeks the Way," what Dogen, the founder of Japanese Soto Zen, calls "the seed of Bodhi."* It is not necessary to go to a special place or to receive something from someone else in order to awaken to this mind. The fact is, all we have to do is recognize that the dissatisfaction we feel, the very things that can drive us to pleasure-seeking or spiritual diversion, is the Way-seeking mind.

---

*"Bodhi" means "enlightenment," so awakening the Way-seeking mind is to cultivate the seed of Bodhi. Dogen says that recognizing and following the Way-seeking mind is enlightenment itself.

This recognition is the first step to being centered in ourselves and staying put to face ourselves.

In Buddhism, wisdom is sometimes symbolized by a flaming orb, called the "nyoi jewel," that is guarded by a dragon. To obtain the jewel and find wisdom, we must face that dragon. But the dragon is not off in some far away mystic realm; the dragon is our own existence. Awakening to the Way-seeking mind is the first step in acquiring wisdom. Cultivating this mind in all aspects of daily life is the next step. Facing ourselves down at the deepest levels and fully engaging the most trying difficulties in life with honesty and openness is how we face the dragon. It is only when we stop running from ourselves that we can accomplish this vital work. In time we discover that the jewel of wisdom is ours naturally, and the dragon is the power inherent in our own lives. Recognizing the opportunities to do this work in everyday life has been a recurring theme in my efforts as a priest.

To further understand the Zen tradition, and to understand why finding opportunities for practice in everyday life has been important, it helps to realize that Zen grew out of traditional Buddhism, which venerates the monk as a renunciate. In traditional Buddhism, the monk leaves the world and all its involvements to find an inner truth. What Zen does is to bring the Buddhist renunciate back into ordinary, everyday life, but with a new perspective. Shaking off the "stench of enlightenment," a Zen monk wishes to live in harmony with the everyday world, with "no trace of the inner life to be caught." Nonetheless, life in a Zen temple is quite different from that of typical lay practitioners, and in the larger monasteries, the monks devote nearly all their time to formal practice. Many who wish to follow the way of Zen find it hard to believe that it can be done in their own lives, just as they are.

I had spent ten years in a Zen monastery, and Gyokuko seven, when we got married in 1982 and moved to Portland, Oregon, taking on our little city temple here. The monastery we came from was steeped in the renunciate tradition. Life there was very monastic, one could say "cloistered," and other-worldly. Moving from a rural monastery in the mountains of Northern California to an urban temple that focused on lay practice was quite a challenge. At first we felt as if we had landed on another planet. In the midst of city life, with its pace, noise, and aggression, it seemed that our practice was foreign; that it took place only within our little temple, and "outside" we just survived. We also had to learn that a city temple was simply not going to work like a monastery. That's something we're still learning years later. While I've come to see that there is no fundamental difference between practicing as a monk or a layman, the form the practice takes is very different. Learning to adapt the monastic forms, and learning to answer the questions that arise in lay life, took much more listening than talking. Weekly classes, articles in our newsletter *Still Point*, and long talks with members became the forum for a dialogue through which we all learned and are still learning.

A Zen monastery is a remarkable place to be, and the opportunities for learning in one are wonderful. Spending time in a monastery can help clarify our intentions and aspirations. But other than the monastic forms, the basic elements that are used in the teaching are nothing other than ordinary, everyday life. These are the same elements found in life in a city or a suburb. The dialogue that has instructed Gyokuko and me in how to organize a city temple for lay practice revolves around this point. This dialogue, and all that we learned from it, is what this book is all about.

Over the years, Gyokuko and I have also been instructed by the lessons learned at other centers and by the writings that have come out of them. In particular, I would like to acknowledge the influence of the Second Generation Zen Teachers' Conference, an annual gathering of people whose training was primarily here in North America and who are now heads of temples. That gathering and the contacts made through it have been invaluable to us in refining the program here. As Zen develops in this country, I have come to see each center as an independent experiment in adapting the practice to this setting. I look forward to more talks with teachers at those centers, and to reading the expressions of the Dharma that develop there. It is in this spirit that I offer this book. I hope that some may find it useful.

CONTENTS

THE MIND THAT
SEEKS THE WAY

WHY ZAZEN?

Sometimes I get a blank look; sometimes an incredulous stare. It's almost always a conversation stopper. It happens every time I find myself explaining to someone, who really only asked to be polite, that I am a Zen Buddhist priest, and that I engage in a religious practice of sitting stock still for thirty minutes or more, gazing at a blank wall. The brave-hearted of these surprised people recover and press on with the conversation, but my little bombshell has produced some wonderfully befuddled looks. After one such exchange, I got to musing about how I could explain the basic idea behind this practice in very general terms that would be easy to comprehend, and it occurred to me that almost everyone has some experience of what it is we "Zen people" are trying to do.

When asked, most people would say that what they really want out of life is simply to be happy and fulfilled. But when we try to list the elements that would comprise these goals, they aren't so easy to figure out. Happiness in life is much more than just being in a good mood. Consider the way some people like to cry at movies. Superficially, this makes no sense, yet they find it emotionally satisfying. Elements of a rich, full, satisfying life include challenge, achievement, growth, loving relationships, and giving of ourselves. But a truly successful life also includes equanimity and peace of mind, a sense of perspective in the face of both success and failure, love and loss. For no matter how much we may gain in life, it is certain that we will all face loss at various times. And it is very hard to accept the one with equanimity while clinging desperately to the other.

Zen meditation is the practice of sitting very still once or twice a day. In temples the periods are thirty to fifty minutes long, but just a few moments done regularly is good too. In the Soto Zen tradition, meditation is done facing a blank wall. This practice is called zazen, and while it is very simple, it has profound effects difficult to describe. Even someone who has never tried the practice can imagine what sitting still everyday would be like. The effort it takes to really sit still is amazingly revealing, for each desire to fidget, each time our minds wander off, tells us something about ourselves. One function of meditation is to open our eyes to seeing ourselves, and everything around us, in the clearest possible way. But its greater purpose is to help us be in touch with our own center, a place deep within ourselves that we feel to be still, peaceful, and full of bliss; or sometimes it is solid, immovable, stable; and sometimes dynamic, powerful, and flowing. It can be all of these things, and more.

When you get away from it all in the mountains or the desert, or out on a sailboat perhaps, where it is quiet and peaceful, where the phone doesn't ring and there are no deadlines, it is very easy to feel at peace with the world and to know who you are. At such times, everything seems possible. But, when you are harried and busy, and especially when things go wrong, you can experience a kind of identity crisis. At times like these it is easy to lose track of who you are, and what you really feel. This is because we have a tendency to identify ourselves with our objectives, goals, careers, etc., and where we think we are going in life. When those things are in chaos and not working out at all, who are we? One way to describe meditation is taking the time to remember who we are in complete silence. Someone once said that those who are the most successful in their careers are those who are best able to keep their work in perspective. Meditation is a practice that puts your whole life—everything—into perspective. So I suppose you could say that it is a key to being successful, in the deepest sense, in life itself.

Meditation is a discipline because you cannot depend upon quiet mountainsides or a trip to the seashore for your peace of mind. Besides, you quickly find out that when you are really distracted, even that won't work. Meditation is the practice of finding the still point of balance within your own being in the midst of all kinds of conditions. Its purpose is not to escape, not to duck responsibility or involvement in daily life, but to know with certainty exactly where the center of your own being is. When we remember who we are in silence, we bring tremendous strength and insight to daily life. The perspective gained through meditation in ordinary daily life is a key to a truly successful life, but it is also a powerful means of progressing on the spiritual path. It brings inner peace of mind and helps us discover how to live in harmony with everything around us, at home, at work, and even in the difficult social and political world in which we find ourselves.

> *The water flows from the high mountains,*
> *seeking its own way, to the level ground.*
> *This is Buddha-Dharma. Buddha-Dharma is the*
> *Great Natural Way. The rain falls, the wind blows.*[1]

CREATE A DESTINY

In Stanley Kubrick's *2001—A Space Odyssey*, Mission Commander David Bowman finds his voyage taking a cosmic turn. In a series of scenes, he catches a glimpse of someone, across a room perhaps. When he turns to look, he meets the eyes of an older man, himself, looking back. The perspective changes to show the view of the older man looking back to where the younger man had been but now has vanished. It is a beautiful depiction of those moments when we realize we have aged.

Not long ago I was running in a local park. I came upon a fellow jogger, running hard, coming toward me. He was somewhat overweight and had a thick moustache, so it was a moment or two before I recognized that he was about ten years younger than I. As we passed each other it struck me that I used to pace myself faster, the way he was running, pushing quite hard. But then I went through a rather long period of injuries and two knee operations, so I eased off, thinking that steady effort for longer periods everyday would work better while I recuperated. But now, seeing the youthful quality in the younger man's stride, I realized that I just don't run like that anymore. I saw very clearly that I had aged.

It was a very interesting moment. Such insights in the past were always ones of recognizing an increase in my capabilities; I was coming of age, getting stronger, becoming more capable. This time, being in my forties, I saw clearly that I have slowed down physically, and that my desire to push so hard has subsided. Running in opposite directions, the younger man and I met again on the far side of the park. But now, instead of running, he was walking and out of breath. What a surprise. It just goes to show that over time, if we keep up our training, we can make real progress, improving in many ways, rather than simply losing youthful energy. We can't hold back the clock, of course, and this is not really the point of what I have to say. The point is this: when we undergo Zen practice we are often unaware of its effects until those moments when we look back and see how far we have come. The first year or two, things can happen rather quickly; the practice is new, and we are making discoveries almost every week. But later, nothing much seems to happen. In the long run, daily practice is like daily exercise. The changes are so gradual that we are unaware of them.

I read somewhere a bit of advice a dog trainer would give to owners of large breed puppies: never encourage a little puppy to do things you don't want a 90-pound dog to do. It's cute when a cuddly little puppy curls up on the sofa, nibbles on your fingers, or jumps up on you to get your attention. But this is not endearing behavior in a very large dog. What does this have to do with the Buddhadharma? Simply this. We all age, but how we do it is a product of the choices we make throughout life. Many things that can be attractive in the young do not wear well with age. At the same time, maturity, stability, and wisdom are qualities that grow only when we cultivate them. They do not come automatically with time. The fact of the matter is, young quirky people grow into old quirky people, set in their quirky ways; unless they choose otherwise. Zen practice means to induce changes in ourselves, and so to remain mentally open and flexible. With this comes inner stability rather than outer rigidity, discernment and wisdom rather than opinionated belief. Mental flexibility means we can continue to grow, to really mature, with a stability far different from being set in our ways. There is an old Buddhist saying:

> Form a thought, create an impulse.
> Form an impulse, create an action.
> Form an action, create a habit.
> Form a habit, create a destiny.

Zen practice, as with all spiritual paths, is a process of becoming. It begins with a thought: "I want to improve my life," or "There must be something more to life than this." From this the impulse to practice arises. But unless we follow up on this impulse and really do something about it, we fall back into well-worn patterns and the "thought of enlightenment" remains a wistful, distant dream.

While the ultimate purpose of Zen reflects the human heart's highest aspiration, the arena of Zen practice is right here in everyday life. It is really the little things we do, the choices we make today, moment by moment, that determine who we will be tomorrow. Grand gestures once in a while do little to affect what we become. We may hold lofty ideals of tolerance, but if we spend much of our time griping and complaining, what are we in the process of becoming? When we cheat a little because it is the "norm," what are we accomplishing? Many people these days feel that their lives are out of their own control. They feel powerless in the face of the forces around them. But was there ever a time when this was not the case? Stone Age tribes were certainly no less at the mercy of their environment than we are today. Powerlessness and hopelessness are feelings that arise from within, and it is from within that they can be addressed. The same is true of greed, anger, and despair. The message of Zen is that when we feel the impulse, the "thought of enlightenment," it is the stirring of the mind that seeks the Way, and, at that very moment, the power to change our lives is in our hands. The means to this change is practice. It begins with a first step: creating an action. It follows through with regular, sustained effort: creating a habit. It finds completion in continual awakening. Through practice we create a destiny, an inner destiny of wisdom, stability, and peace of mind.

An Honest Doubt

There is more faith in an honest doubt,
Believe me, than in half the creeds.
                              Tennyson[2]

The necessity of faith in religious life and practice is something the "faithful" take for granted. The "Awakening of Faith"[3] is considered an essential step in Buddhism, and while Zen may be thought of as nonconformist by some, on this point there really can be no disagreement. After all, taking up a practice that leads towards "enlightenment," a state that cannot be known until experienced, implies a faith that such an experience really does exist. Yet faith, as understood in Buddhism, is a very simple thing. It is gentle, flexible, and does not depend upon belief systems. We can see examples of faith like this in operation all around us if we look. It finds expression in a positive and gentle attitude towards life, and is identical with the acceptance that lies at the base of everything positive we do.

Faith as the basis of everyday actions? Many people would find that absurd, if not insulting. We want to believe that the choices we make are essentially rational ones. We tend to think that others, society in general, the whole world even, behaves that way. But when you think about it, the rational process comes a long way behind more gut level feelings as a basis for everyday behavior. How much reason is involved in a purchase of clothing, a record album, a set of dishes, even a house or car? When we feel hungry, how much of our desire is for calories, and how much is for Chinese food, or Mexican food? Economies and political structures rise and fall on intangibles like hope and confidence, or anxiety and fear of loss. Consider something even more basic. We drive on busy highways with nothing separating us from oncoming traffic but a line painted on the road. We will step out into an intersection with oncoming traffic in full view, with nothing to stop the cars but a red light on top of a pole. In these situations it is, I think, more a matter of trusting that the drivers of those cars hurtling towards us want, and will tend to act, in their own self-interest. Without that trust it would be impossible for us to step off the curb, or to keep our minds on the business of controlling our own cars when driving. But underneath this trust is a deep intuition. In these situations we sense that other people, at their very core, think and feel much the same way we do. Accepting that is an act of faith. This simple kind of faith, forming the foundation of action in everyday life, is really the same faith that opens the door to the experience of complete unity with the entire universe. Like fish within the great ocean, we are at all times sustained and supported by this unity. We can never be separate from it, yet we are usually ignorant of it. Realizing this unity is the mystical experience of Zen. Awakening to simple, positive faith is a first step.

While we may not be quite so rational as we would like to believe, faith is much more natural to us than we think. This very natural faith requires no strain, just a little acceptance. So what is this "honest doubt" that Tennyson connects with faith? To hold an honest doubt is to want to know, above all, what is true. It is not negative skepticism to ask "Is my understanding of this correct?" or, "Is this really what it represents itself to be?" An honest doubt, with a little humility, is necessary for the recognition that Truth is so immense, so vast, that our understanding of it can only be quite small. While humbling, this recognition leaves us open to endless possibilities. In comparison, a negative, skeptical doubt is confining because with it we lose the sense of wonder so essential for uncovering what is not yet known. With an honest doubt we wish to understand, but not to limit other people, or other ways of understanding and expressing the Truth. So often a "creed" carries the implication "This is the Truth. Therefore, all else must be false." Belief in such a creed can squeeze out the space for asking, "What is True? Do I really understand?" It seems to me that when belief becomes rigid, without gentleness and flexibility, without room for honest doubt, real faith ceases to exist.

With an honest doubt we can recognize the imperfections in things, weigh them against their merits, and understand the value of a teaching or a practice. Eventually an honest doubt, along with gentle faith, will lead to an understanding of the real perfection that lies hidden in all things. Religious traditions, and Zen is no different, are made up of individuals with strengths and weaknesses, faults and foibles, and, of course, the potential for enlightenment. If faith permits us to see enlightenment manifesting around us and in the actions of others, honest doubt permits us to accept human nature as it is. The miracle of transformation that Zen training works upon us requires both of these. Gently accepting our own limitations, we can at last come to know enlightenment at work within ourselves too. To understand honest doubt, though, there is something else to consider. An honest doubt is one that is directed inwardly as much, if not more so, than it is toward outward things. To hold an honest doubt is to first say to oneself, "I could be wrong," and then to admit, on the other hand, that "They could be wrong, too."

When I was in training at the monastery, I noticed that sometimes people would arrive with unbridled enthusiasm and intensity. But often that enthusiasm would dry up in a day or two, and off they would go in search of something else. I remember one man, a university student, who arrived at the gate in the afternoon and announced that he had given up everything. He had come to spend the rest of his life in meditation at the monastery. All this without ever having visited or even written to the monastery before. He was sent to join me digging holes in the garden, which was part of our effort to put in a new septic system. I dug my holes, but his mind was elsewhere. He wanted to talk about Zen. He wanted me to understand how deeply he felt about becoming a monk. He was gone before dinner. His was a rather extreme case, perhaps, for he had the drive and the desire for enlightenment, born of dissatisfaction with his life. But he did not have the patience, the sense of direction, and the caution that comes with an honest doubt. Those seeking a "quick fix" will soon be disappointed with the simple practice of training within everyday life, and so they quickly set off to search for something else.

"When people stop believing in God, the problem is not that thereafter they believe in nothing, it is that thereafter they will believe in anything."

I once heard this remark, attributed to G.K. Chesterton, English essayist and novelist, and I was struck by his observation that people will, despite protestations to the contrary, tend to hang their faith on some sort of belief system. On this subject, Chesterton wrote:

> Unless that part of the mind is satisfied by a faith it will be satisfied by a fad: those who have destroyed a church have only created a sect.[4]

Today, instead of "sect," he no doubt would have used the word "cult." Chesterton wrote very skillfully about how our underlying belief systems, conscious or not, affect the way we live our lives.[5] He then concluded that it is important to choose our belief system carefully. While I agree with him in part, there is a big difference between believing a "revealed Truth," and believing we can discover what is True. Nonetheless, his observations put a finger on something with regard to this matter of faith and doubt that I think is important. And that is, without the flexibility of seeking implied in an honest doubt, we are impaled on the necessity of belief. To me, belief can be a very formidable obstacle. Faith with an honest doubt is open ended, as we constantly search for what is true. When a religious "faith" demands rigid belief without any doubt, the element of seeking for the Truth is gone. Without seeking, how can there be a spiritual path? To me, real faith embraces honest doubt and requires very little in the way of belief. So often, when people throw off the yoke of one rigid set of beliefs, they flounder about, grasping first after this, then after that, like the fellow who came to the monastery to spend the rest of his life. Perhaps this explains why people turn to newspaper horoscopes, or authoritarian sects, religious or political, which offer all the answers in neat, simple packages. They trade one yoke for another before they realize what they have done, and this is what Chesterton saw. Simple faith and all-acceptance, with an honest doubt, can be very difficult to balance, but it is the only formula I can see for a truly spiritual life. It is my belief that real faith cannot exist without honest doubt, for without it we loose the humility and flexibility to seek the Truth.

Great Master Dogen, who brought Soto Zen from China to Japan, taught that the mind that seeks the Way, that wishes to know the Truth, is the Buddha Mind itself.[6] To seek the Way. What a beautiful expression of enlightenment. It is full of faith, for it seeks an understanding that can only come with experience. It holds an honest doubt, for it is full of the humility to know we must always seek the Truth. Dogen also taught that to live by Zen is simply to follow the Wayseeking mind in a normal, everyday life. This means to live morally, and to cultivate charity, tenderness, benevolence, and sympathy in all the everyday ways our own lives present to us at work, at home, with friends, family, and with others who seek the Way. This sums up the essence of teaching and practice in Soto Zen. Why do we practice and teach in such a simple, even mundane, way? It would actually be much easier to provide all the answers than to point the way for each to find the Truth for himself or herself in their own everyday lives. Or, as an option, we could mystify, bamboozle, or intimidate rather than instruct. If you emphasize how difficult Zen is to understand, and underline all the reasons why people cannot understand, you get yourself off the hook when they don't understand. Mystification tends to be the Zen "creed" that gets in the way of simple faith with an honest doubt. But Zen practice is really very simple. It consists of meditation, moral precepts, and sincerity. Within such a practice, deep faith and realization arise very naturally. Why? Because along with the simple faith that we can, in fact, understand, the necessity of questioning with an honest doubt is not only recognized, it is encouraged. What mystery could withstand such a combination?

ALONE IN THE DARK

"If we are all enlightened from the very start, why bother with all this?" The man sitting across from me gestured around the room to indicate he was speaking of the Zen Center itself. A good question. We had been speaking of the Zen teaching that we are all naturally one with enlightenment from the beginning. Therefore, enlightenment is not something to be gained, nor is it something we produce. Instead, as we are one with it always, we need only realize it. Great Master Dogen had exactly the same question when he left Japan to study Zen in China. In the first essay he wrote after returning to Japan, he set out to answer that very question. "The Way is essentially perfect and exists everywhere. There is no need either to seek or to realize the Way," he wrote. "Essentially the Truth is very close to you; is it then necessary to run around in search of it?" Then he adds, "Even so, if there is the slightest error, there is a gulf as great as that between heaven and earth. If so much as a thought of agreeable or disagreeable arises, one becomes confused."[7] It appears that this question is one that monks and laymen have pondered over for a good many years.

Dogen speaks of our daily lives as "training" and says that this training is enlightenment. We can understand this by comparing enlightenment to the law of gravity. We can never be separate from the law of gravity; we are always one with it, no matter what we do. We express our oneness with it perfectly whether we fall on our faces, walk across the room, or flow in the graceful movements of a dance. As Dogen says, the daily life of Zen is training, in which we learn to harmonize our lives with the Truth, just as in learning to walk or dance, we learn to move in harmony with the law of gravity. When we refuse to accept the need for training, our enlightenment manifests as endless karmic consequences; like the floor, the Truth will come up to hit us in the face.

"Alright," the man said, "I can see the necessity of learning to train myself. But what is the purpose of joining a sangha, or of taking a teacher? Would it not be better to look within myself instead of to people and things outside myself?" Another good question. The Truth is always with us, and it appears naturally in our own experience. It is also a tenet of Zen that we should not seek to gain the Truth from others, for this would be to miss seeing it within ourselves. So why do we take teachers and join sanghas? Just as the truth of Zen is unobscured and available to us, so are Newton's principles of physics, or the theory of relativity. Nothing stands between us and any truth. But why is it we resist learning from others when it comes to matters of inner Truth, yet understand perfectly the necessity of learning mathematics or physics from those qualified to teach them? A university is a storehouse of knowledge gained in the world of measurement and calculation. A religious tradition such as Soto Zen is an institution that embodies and protects the wisdom of the ages known as Buddhism.

The law of gravity is obvious, wouldn't you say? But it wasn't obvious at all until it was pointed out and clearly explained by Newton. So great was his contribution to mathematics and physics that others praised him as the greatest mind of his age. Someone once asked him why it was that he towered above all the other great scientists of his day. "If I seem to be farther than others," he replied, "it is because I stand upon the shoulders of giants." Newton studied the scientific knowledge of his time long and hard, as did Einstein, and each added his own insight to that which went before. Shakyamuni Buddha was no different. He had the humility to seek the Truth from the greatest sages of his age, and he received the seal from each. His contribution was to discover the practice of the Middle Way and the meditation we call "just sitting." These practices form the gateway to inner discovery. From the Middle Way and "just sitting" as fountainhead, all the teachings of Buddhism have come forth, over thousands of years. The wisdom it embodies is deep and broad, subtle and fathomless. We can make it our own through our efforts at practice. We discover it for ourselves, within ourselves, through practice. But why reinvent the wheel? A tradition like Soto Zen represents the combined experience of generations who have learned from mistakes as well as success.

We take a teacher because she or he holds the lineage of a tradition. We take refuge in the whole Buddhist Sangha because the wisdom of

Buddhism is far greater than that held by any individual. Within the tradition called Soto Zen, this wisdom is nurtured and protected even today. In the master-disciple relationship, each person finds the Truth for themselves *via* a direct pointing by the teacher. The disciple's wisdom will also grow through association with others on the path, for all of us come to express the Truth in our own unique ways. Seeing this helps the disciple recognize how much greater the Truth is than just one person's experience. What can possibly compare with this? Inner wisdom cannot develop without humility, so how could it be possible to find the Truth while refusing the teaching? Without a good teacher and wise sangha, we are sitting alone in the dark. How could we ever imagine the shape of a face or the color of our own eyes?

Shakyamuni Buddha once said, "All paths lead to the goal. Walk that one which is best for you." The way of Soto Zen is not an exclusive path to the Truth. Today, you can find Soto, Rinzai, Korean Chogye, and Vietnamese Zen Temples right here in North America. There are also Tibetan and Theravadin teachers here. Some temples are primarily for monks, others for laymen. Each offers a tried and true method of training, but each is just one out of many. These days the number of religious paths seems endless. Making a commitment to a group, however, and becoming part of a sangha is very important, whichever path you choose. When we decide to practice with others, we are beginning to recognize that the most difficult obstacles to overcome are our own delusions. Like a smudge on the face, they remain unseen without a mirror. It is our relationship with others, particularly in the context of religious training, that gives us the chance to see ourselves clearly. If our relationship to the ground helps us understand our oneness with gravity, our relationships to a sangha and a teacher help us understand our oneness with enlightenment. So these are the reasons for joining with others and taking a teacher; they help us understand and manifest the Truth within ourselves.

SOME VERY SHORT STORIES ON THE SUBJECT OF TRAVEL

GETTING STARTED

Imagine a guy who is shopping for a new car. He reads about them in *Consumer Reports* and automotive magazines, and he talks with mechanics and friends who own cars. He does a lot of shopping and test driving and learns about the different models offered by Honda, Toyota, Ford, and the others, and he studies their different characteristics and features. He learns about ease of maintenance, costs of parts, and where the good mechanics are. In time he becomes a pretty good source of information on the relative strengths and weaknesses of cars available on the dealers' lots. Then it suddenly occurs to him, "Gee, if I actually buy one of these cars, I'll spend all my time driving the one I own. I'll get locked into just that one and lose the valuable insights I gain by testing and comparing them all. Besides, in the deepest sense all cars serve the same end, so if I choose one I will be denying all the others. That would be a real shame, so I guess I'll just continue doing what I'm doing."

What this guy has obviously forgotten is that the purpose of buying a car is to use it to get somewhere. The same is true of spiritual practices. Making a commitment to one particular spiritual vehicle is very similar to making a choice about buying a car. In this story, making a choice would mean that our friend would lose his impartial perspective, because the specific knowledge he would gain about the car he chooses would come at the expense of the overview he has held on the many choices available. However, what he would learn about the one he chooses would go so much deeper than the superficial, general knowledge he had before. But this is still beside the point. What he would really gain by choosing and then using one specific car is getting to his real destination. It is not until he finally uses the car in just this way that he will truly understand that the differences between the various models really don't matter much at all. Merely thinking that they are all the same anyway is just an excuse not to make a commitment to one, thereby avoiding getting started on the journey. Until he takes one all the way, he will not really understand this.

This little story may sound pretty silly, but it is amazing how often this point is missed with regard to spiritual practices. It is important to shop around; at least enough to find a vehicle that truly suits you. But after a while reading and comparing material from various traditions has less and less value. It is not until after you are well on the journey for yourself that such comparisons become helpful again. Then they can be inspirational and add insight to your own practice. It is said in Mahayana Buddhism that each form of religious practice is like a raft that can carry you to the "other shore." But after crossing the river, only a fool carries the raft on his back. And so it is. But without taking up the raft in the first place, there can be no arriving at the "other shore."

ON THE ROAD

Now imagine that in time the careful consumer in our last story realizes that what he really wants to do is to get to "New York." So he bites the bullet and buys a car. It's not perfect, but what the heck, it suits him pretty well. He has heard from some who claim to have seen this exotic place that "New York" lies on the far side of the continent, past great mountains and vast plains, some 3,000 miles toward the rising sun. He finds some maps that show the way and sets off down the road. Like all new adventures, this one is great fun—for a while. But somewhere into the second or third day our traveler finds his back is tired, his shoulders ache, and his eyes are bleary from staring at that little white line. Boring!!! This was supposed to be a journey of great discovery making life much better, not just cramped monotony! "This has got to be the wrong road," he thinks, "I'd better go back and figure out where I went wrong." So back he goes to Portland to think things through.

Our traveller is a bit discouraged for a while, but he thinks about it and decides that next time he must be more careful to pick the right road. He studies the maps and settles on a more southerly route. This time around he's not so fussy about the cramped posture, but gad, the heat! "This will kill me if it gets much worse," he says to himself. So, back to Portland once more. Think it over; study the map; start again. This time out it's a terribly rough road, with detours and potholes and he breaks an axle. So, after many starts and much hardship, here he sits, still in Portland.

Sounds a little like the foolishness about buying the car in the first place, doesn't it; and it is. But this takes the problem a little further. When we actually do get started on a spiritual path, there is one thing we can be sure of, and that is running into difficulty. In fact, it is absolutely essential that we do. The purpose of taking the path is to find a place that lies beyond the "self." But to do this requires that we transcend the "self," and for this we must, of course, face the "self." This part is never easy, and it makes up the difficult portions of the trip to "New York."

So often people get started on a spiritual path and stay on it as long as it is enjoyable. But as soon as the going gets rough, they bail out thinking that "Something must be wrong here," or "Perhaps this path wasn't the right one after all," or "This aspect of the practice just isn't right for me." Sometimes they will take a bit of this practice, a bit of that one, and put together a "path" with no rough spots. This is always a real shame because their path consists of a series of first steps, with no progression into the areas that really matter. After some time of doing this, they may notice that they have traveled much further than 3,000 miles but never got to any such place as "New York." So obviously, they figure, "New York" was just someone's fantasy all along.

Commitment and follow-through on a spiritual path will lead to a deep understanding of that path. Various paths may diverge, taking people following them in different, even opposite, directions at times. But these differences are like switchbacks on a mountainside. All true paths still lead upward and so converge again toward the mountaintop. Only by taking one path all the way can we gain the insight into what taking another path might have been like. We live in an age in which commitment is not greatly valued. Marriages and careers seem to last as long as they are entertaining. If we fear being limited by making a commitment, we can end up paralyzed by our own freedom of choice. Fearing that we will lose some new option that may come along or that changing fashion may cause us to be poorly judged by others, we avoid following through on wonderful opportunities that present themselves to us. This is really sad to see.

The Buddha advised us that all true paths lead to the same goal. But we must pick one, after all, and walk it. The Zen way of endless practice is to open the mind to "always becoming Buddha." Peace of mind arises as we realize that we are enlightened from the start, and there is nothing to be achieved. "New York" was right here all along. But we can't know that without taking the practice deeply into every-day life, and this is actually getting on the road. What can these contradictory images mean? In this paradox we have one meaning of the koan of the "gateless gate."*

EATING DUST

On a hot, dusty, and very sticky afternoon in mid-July, a car is barreling down a dirt road. All of a sudden the driver realizes he is going the wrong way! He slams on the brakes, comes to a stop, and. . . . BLECHH!! . . . the car is enveloped in a cloud of dust. It fills the driver's eyes and nose, combines with sweat to form wet, muddy streaks on his face and arms, and he realizes that he has to drive back through the cloud, which hangs over the road for miles.

People often ask why it is that not long after starting to meditate and train within the Precepts, things seem to get much worse. Their emotions get churned up, their minds become a cacophony of noise, they experience weird pains and things moving about inside of them.

---

*It is said that to enter the mind of Zen is to pass through the "Gateless Barrier." This is also the name of a famous set of koans, or mind awakening questions based on the stories of ancient masters.

Then for good measure all sorts of stray and painful oddities turn up in their lives, right out of the blue, seemingly for no reason at all. Before we begin to practice, we are often able to breeze along quite nicely without being aware of the karma we are generating. But it rises up behind us like a cloud of dust, getting bigger and bigger. And karmic consequence can be much more substantial than a cloud of dust. It can eventually develop into a tidal wave that overtakes us and comes crashing down with tremendous force. These are times that life really knocks us about and can seem terribly unfair. But we have the choice of realizing our own responsibility for our situation instead of just whining "Why me?"

Starting on the path of Zen practice can actually precipitate the reaping of karmic consequences because it involves the realization that we have to change the way we have been doing things. So we stop barreling the wrong way down the dirt road and. . . . Wham! . . . our karma catches up with us. But later, heading the right way back up the road, we often think "I'm going the right way now! Why am I still eating dust?"

So many times in life, especially when we don't understand why unpleasant things are happening to us, we have to just be patient and realize that these things will, eventually, die down on their own. For many years I approached life by gritting my teeth, putting my head down, and butting my way through obstacles. I even tried to train as a monk that way. At one point I suffered an injury to my back. It improved slowly through exercise, but I had constant, chronic pain in my hips, and sciatica in one leg. But I didn't let it slow me down. I would grit my teeth and charge straight ahead. To do that, though, I had to block out awareness of my own body, for ignoring the pain meant ignoring my own back and legs. If you aren't paying attention to your body, you can't move about in a place as crowded as the community room at the monastery where I trained without crashing into things. Pretty soon I began dropping things, too. Before long I had developed a reputation for being clumsy and fumble-fingered. Whenever something would fall with a crash, someone would call, "Kyogen? Is that you?" It became quite funny to everyone but me. But the situation forced me to consider very carefully why this was happening. In time I began to recognize what I was doing, and I slowly learned to accept my physical discomfort with more gentle awareness. Things changed very quickly as I learned this lesson, and I soon got over my clumsiness. But my reputation lingered on. Even though in time I was no more prone to accidents than other monks, my name remained associated with every loud crash. When I occasionally did bump into something, it would be pointed to as proof that Kyogen couldn't walk through an open door. I began to resent this quite a bit, and then to argue the point. But my resistance only put a spotlight on the issue. Eventually I realized that I was just going to have to eat dust for a while. It took about a year, but in time it all died away. As I stopped resisting, my back began to improve rapidly too. In an odd way I appreciate what happened because it is only by seeing clearly how we generate karma that we come to know ourselves well. There are times when tenacious determination is a genuine asset, but making a habit of butting my head against walls was doing me no good. It took a period of eating dust to see that clearly, and to learn that patience is an essential element in deepening practice.

Success & Timeless Values

Much of the early 1980s was a time of economic recession in the US. Anyone who lived in Oregon back then also knows that the economic recovery enjoyed in many parts of the country later that decade was not spread very evenly across the country or society as a whole. In Oregon things didn't turn around until the very late 1980s. During the worst of that recession, Americans finally faced the fact that many industries, even whole segments of the economy, would never regain the robust good health they enjoyed in the 50s and 60s. This was certainly the case in Oregon, where whole industries cut back drastically. Chronic unemployment and the struggle to find new ways of making a living were a fact of life for many people formerly employed in those industries. It was traumatic for the whole country to watch media coverage of their plight while they tried to cope with these problems day in and day out. Recognition of the profound effects this could have on their self-esteem began to grow. For the whole population in those days, there was growing apprehension and doubt about the future. As a priest, these issues sometimes came up when members consulted me about practice, and I found many of them surprised that I would have any personal understanding of what they were going through.

When Gyokuko and I first came to Oregon in 1982, we were filling in for another priest, a citizen of Switzerland, who needed to take a leave of absence to straighten out a snafu concerning his status in this country. His life eventually took a new direction, and that is how we came to take the position here permanently. While we were filling in that first year, we felt it was important that the temple not be burdened with the greater expense of supporting two of us. The temple was very small back then, and those were lean years. Therefore, we decided it was necessary for one or both of us to take on work outside the temple to make ends meet. This happened just at the low point of the recession, and entering the job market right then proved very educational. I had put myself through college doing temporary or part-time work. While it could be tough finding good work in those days too, I quickly found out that things are very different when you apply for "grunt work" like that once you get into your thirties. It didn't take long for me to understand firsthand what it can be like for someone trying to start over. During hard times, conscientious, hard-working people can find themselves unemployed through no fault of their own, and many of them, try as they will, won't find work for a long time. During the 80s, even executives, once on the fast track to high paying upper management, found themselves derailed by the plight of contracting industries that had to cut back at all levels just to survive. Just as I was in the middle of this and looking for work, I ran across an article that made note of this problem as it pertains to executives. It pointed out that in business circles, there was a growing awareness that they needed to expand their understanding of the word "success." The American image of a successful man or woman is of one who, through indomitable will, overcomes all obstacles to achieve their goals, usually of greater and greater wealth. This is the classic American image of a "winner," which carries with it the belief that there are types of people that win, and others that lose. Apparently, according to the article, the realization was dawning in corporate America that resiliency in the face of setbacks is also an important quality in a successful person. The article went on to say that it was a major change of thinking in the business world to recognize elements of success in a non-winning situation. But it is not just those in the corporate board rooms of this country that have suffered from a simplistic view of winning and losing. As a culture, we have all tended to think this way, and such attitudes about success, failure, and personal worth merit some close attention. I think that looking at it from the perspective of meditation and Zen practice can be quite helpful.

Through my own experience back in 1982-83, I was able to see for myself just how much a recession is an attitude of mind. I also saw how this group "mind-set" could magnify the effects of being unemployed on an individual. In times of expansion, when they are full of faith in the future, people act with confidence and trust in others. In hard times, anxiety about the future leads people to clutch at what they have and to lose confidence in themselves and other people. An example often cited is that, fearing that things could get worse, people become reluctant to spend or invest, and thereby amplify the trend; but this is just one aspect of it. A job hunter during a resession experiences this in a significant and very personal way that can trigger despair and great doubt about self-worth. Zen practice opens a door onto something that lies far beyond any external measure of success or self-worth. During this recession I learned firsthand how important that can be.

One thing I noticed is that in times of high unemployment or economic uncertainty, employers begin to count things against a job seeker when they could just as well count them in his favor. For example, an unemployed factory worker in a troubled industry with a good work record and years of service, perhaps with responsibilities as a foreman, would seem to have that in his favor when applying for work. But instead, the prospective employer chooses to consider him a poor risk for long-term employment since he could well return to his former job if the industry recovers. Why does she do this? The fact is, when there are many applicants for each opening, the employer has to eliminate all but one. So she quickly falls into the pattern of trying to see each applicant from a negative point of view. When I was looking for work, I would follow any lead. I decided I would not turn up my nose at anything, because any honorable part-time job that brought in a few dollars would do. I remember one moment very clearly when I turned up to see about part-time work at a gas station. The manager bit down on his cigar, looked me over skeptically, and said, "What the hell are you doin' here?" I felt like I had a sign around my neck that said, "Approaching middle age and college educated." How, in a situation like that, do you explain that you are a Zen Buddhist priest willing to do part time work to make ends meet? I did my best. I watched the manager's face as the realization grew that he wouldn't have to strain to find a reason to drop me from his list. He smiled and nodded, but I could sense a kind of relief in his response. It was the relief he showed that helped me understand his situation. I looked around at all the young kids there applying for the job, some of them probably high school dropouts, and most of them fairly desperate for any job to get them started. How difficult it must have been for that manager to turn down nine such kids for every one he hired. Job applicants can feel a kind of negative scrutiny turned on them as interviewers subconsciously search for a quick reason to eliminate them. The interviewers don't want to look too long and hard, lest they begin to sympathize. So time and again, applicants feel themselves judged lacking as employers narrow their range of acceptable qualifications and choose to count basically irrelevant things as liabilities. You can see a type of desperation in employers, too, since they must turn down many people for every one they hire. Because this makes their jobs unpleasant, they can become brusque or neglect to return calls they promised to make. Unfortunately, this only heightens the job seekers' feelings that decisions that go against them are personal in nature. This sets up a cycle that perpetuates a growing sense of helplessness, frustration, and despair. It's very much like the gas shortages back in the 1970's. There was no more than a 6%–10% shortfall in gasoline supplies, but it caused massive lines at the pumps and a perception of desperate shortages. In the same way, times of recession can lead to a disproportionate sense of hopelessness, despair, and, in so many, a feeling of personal failure.

How strange it was to be a monk in the midst of all that. Like diving into cold water, I would brace myself before entering the employment office, thick with gloom. In many ways, this experience helped emphasize the meaning of being a monk, and the relationship of practice to daily life, for, of course, it is true that my career is being a monk. It lies beyond any success or failure at landing a job pumping gas or hauling boxes, so my sense of identity and self-worth were not deeply tied to any of those other ways I might have spent my time. But there is something far deeper and more significant about this that I had learned from years of training at the monastery, and that stood out so clearly in this situation. What I had learned is that nothing we do, no matter how well or poorly we do it, has any bearing whatsoever on our truest and deepest identity. In the monastery it made no difference whether we were building buildings, milking goats, writing articles, or giving lectures; it made no difference how good we were with a hammer or how skillful with words. The only real measure of success as a monk was whether or not we were able to bow in all circumstances. By bowing I mean the ability to accept events, letting go of expectations with equanimity, and retaining centeredness and peace of mind. Sometimes a monk might find herself praised for good work. At other times she might see her work undone right before her eyes. Priorities there were constantly pre-empted from one day to the next because there was always a bit more to do than could be managed easily. But the success of a monk was gauged by whether or not he or she could accept each thing that came with bows. Living and training like this is invaluable for finding a place beyond the drifting, wandering world of change and struggle. A monk should become a part of that place, base his or her being in it, and not worry too much about external trivialities. When we do this, how little it matters what someone may think of our work, or our qualifications for a job. An African chieftain, squatting on the floor of his mud hut, has all the dignity and regal bearing of the crowned heads of Europe. When you think about this, it means that although we feel a strong need to do our very best, working to support ourselves or our families and making a contribution to society, our sense of self-worth comes from within; it has very little to do with any external measure of what we may or may not accomplish.

Because the purpose of a monk is to focus on this place beyond changeableness, she is a bit of an outsider to both society and the flow of history. By "history," I mean the various trends of social consciousness that come and go. People sometimes think they make a statement about who they are through their modes of dress, or the way they cut their hair. What an absurd idea. Who are they when the style changes? In the 80s the US was in a conservative mood. Before that there was the "Aquarian Age," and the "revolution." After WWII there was limitless economic opportunity; in the 70s and 80s there was uncertainty and doubt, followed by rampant greed. All these modes of consciousness are just fads that come and go. We put them on and change them like changing our clothes. If a monk is an outsider in some ways, he still has a role in society, and that is to stand as a representative of that place that lies beyond changeableness. His function is to help those who wish to find it and know it within themselves, for ultimately, this is the purpose of each one of us, priest or layman. Our deepest identity is as a seeker of Truth, and this we call a monk. When we live from this place beyond changeableness, we find our own source of positivity and strength. We need not succumb to the cycles of despair and euphoria going on around us. This brings a sense of purpose and of success that really matters, one that can last, and one that can have real benefit in all the affairs of the world as well. It goes beyond the "resiliency in the face of setbacks" being recognized in corporate America during the recession, but at the same time, it can be a tremendous source of that resiliency. More importantly, basing our lives on this place beyond changeableness, finding the monk within, inevitably leads to joy and deep freedom. Even in the midst of turmoil and trouble, it will lead to a certain knowledge of that which has the deepest, most real, and most lasting value.

IN
EVERYDAY
LIFE

SHIPS OF FAME, SHIPS OF GAIN

My teacher used to tell a story about a master and disciple who were on a journey by foot. As they walked along a bluff overlooking a harbor, the disciple suddenly turned to his teacher and asked, "Master, please tell me, why is it that after all my years of practice I have yet to attain the Way?" Gesturing out over the harbor, the master replied, "Ships of fame, ships of gain."[1] Desire for fame and gain is considered to be one of the primary obstacles to understanding, and this story struck a deep chord in me because dreaming of fame and gain is like gazing dreamily out at ships on the horizon. Such desire not only takes us out of the here and now, but should we attain fame and gain, it would serve nothing but the ego.

The practice of meditation involves dropping attachments to thoughts and emotions, in fact everything that arises while sitting. In the same way, the practice of Zen in daily life means learning to recognize and release selfish attachments in every form they may appear. But a question arises: as we drop our attachments to things, to goals, and to fame and gain, what is left to motivate us in the competitive world where careers are found? Ambition in this world is highly regarded. What does ambition mean to a Zen student? Does it have any place in the life of practice?

The word ambition literally means "to go around" and is related to the word "ambulatory." Ambition usually refers to the desire to "excel," which the dictionary defines as surpassing others. This is what upward mobility means when we speak of "getting ahead in the world." In this usage "ambition" expresses the essence of aggressive competitiveness. The dictionary, however, lists as a synonym the word "aspiration," which has the same root as the word "spirit." "Aspiration" literally means to "breathe upon," implying "give life to," and is related to inspiration. When we aspire to something, it means we give our lives, energy, and spirit to it. Desire for the Dharma, then, is aspiration. "Aspiration" is also how we would describe a desire to serve. While similar in one way, in another, aspiration is the exact opposite of selfish ambition. If "ambition" is the motivation to achieve in order to advance oneself, "aspiration" is the desire to achieve so that the self may serve.

To me, the highest aspiration is to be a servant of the Truth. This aspiration arises naturally in everyone eventually and only awaits awakening. This is what we call the mind that seeks the Way, the thought of enlightenment, or the seed of Bodhi, and it is this desire that brings us to study Zen. At our very depths, our identity is just this Way-seeking mind. When the thought of enlightenment arises, it presents a clear opening to the Buddha Mind, and its arising is an expression of enlightenment itself. If you really want to attain the Way, as did the monk in the story, then remember that no matter what else you may do, your true identity is as one who seeks the Truth.

Back in the fifties, the writer Colin Wilson put forward a concept he called the "outsider"[2] in which he said that people find great meaning and power in life when they base their existence outside the flow of history. By "history" he means the changing flow of social conscious-ness. Often we try to define ourselves by the way we think and the opinions we share with others, so that these days an "enlightened point of view" means one that is up on the current way of thinking. But anyone who has lived for very long knows that keeping up with the trends can make you quite dizzy. An outsider, as defined by Wilson, is most often one who embraces a tradition that is itself outside the flow of history and then finds the deepest meaning in life within that tradition. Classic examples of such traditions are the monastic institutions of Europe and Asia, and the wandering ascetics of India, each of which, to one degree or another, lead the practitioner to leave the flow of history by actually leaving society. Some monasteries literally bolt the door on it. In the Zen tradition it is said that a monk or sincere lay trainee should be in the world, but not of it. We do not turn our backs on society but exist within it, so that we may offer the merit of our practice to benefit all living things. This is part of the Bodhisattva vow. A Bodhisattva endeavors to embrace everything that appears in the world within her own meditation, turning her back on nothing. An excellent example of an outsider of this type would be

Mahatma Gandhi. He established a foundation for his life within the tradition of the shramanas. The shramana tradition is very ancient. The Buddha joined it when he left home to study with forest ascetics. Shramanas would leave behind all social obligations of family and caste to live very simply, often in the forest. They begged for alms, taking only what they needed. Gandhi found meaning and took strength from this tradition, yet participated fully in the society of his day and had a profound and lasting impact on it. As Zen trainees, we can watch fashions come and go, we can participate in trends if they are healthy, we can vote and dedicate our time to various causes. However, we must find our identity in something timeless and beyond the whims of fashion. Such a seeker of Truth, existing beyond the flow of history, is the monk in each of us, be we layman or priest.

Great Master Dogen tells us that building a ferry, supplying a bridge, earning a living, and producing goods can be expressions of wisdom that benefit others when not done for selfish fame and gain.[3] Such offerings can express the true meaning of charity. Normal everyday commerce, then, can be a wonderful field for the practice of Zen. When I became a monk, it was the aspiration to find the Truth that lead me to undertake the discipline of training in meditation moment by moment. As my eyes opened to this practice, I found that each breath and every action was deeply significant; each moment, and the action contained in it, had great meaning if I took the time to see it. Washing dishes carefully, making a bed neatly, cleaning the floor well, cutting a board with presence of mind; these became the things that were important for me to do. Within such moment by moment practice, I found meaning and satisfaction in my life just as it was. It seems that when our eyes are fully focused on the present, we are best able to understand the timeless purpose of a monk, outside the flow of history. After a few years at the monastery, however, I started to notice a change. The sense of purpose I found moment by moment in little things began to appear in commitments to larger tasks; not just in cutting each board, but in building the cloister, running the kitchen smoothly, as well as just cleaning each dish carefully. Eventually I found myself organizing the monastery's mail-order Buddhist supply business. Even this complex organizational task, with planning, budgets, and all, could be embraced within my sense of purpose as a monk. To do it well would benefit everyone, and it became another opportunity to manifest the practice. The fact is, there is no inherent conflict between knowing one's true identity outside the flow of history and working in the world for the benefit of self and others.

My own teacher used to tell us about a tom cat she saw in Japan. This poor cat was so battered, beaten, and abused that he completely lost his natural pride. Cats are fastidious creatures that keep themselves immaculately clean and are famous for their displays of dignity. This poor fellow let his fur get matted and grimey, with bits of refuse clinging to it. Instead of dignity, he showed only fear and anxiety. People become puffed up with ego pride, but natural pride is just basic self-respect. It is the inclination to keep clean and presentable. It is to give ourselves, and to expect from others, the basic dignity that is everyone's due. Just as there is natural pride, there is natural ambition. This is the desire to realize our own potential, to develop to the best of our abilities, and to do something with this for the benefit of both self and others. Perhaps the distinction between natural and ego-based ambition is not so easy to see as it is with pride, and, as pointed out in the story, ambition can be a formidable obstacle to Zen practice. But if your wish is to do your best for your family, coworkers, and other living things, then making a contribution to society through your career, or any other aspect of your daily life, will become your means of Bodhisattva practice.

Sometimes we use the word "ambition" to refer to aiming high or taking on a great deal in a project, as in "ambitious undertaking." In this case it does not necessarily imply egotistic competitiveness or aggressiveness. Instead, it can mean doing something fully and wholeheartedly, and putting a lot of energy into it. This type of ambition is more like "aspiration," as in "breathing life into," especially when there is a dedication to practice. My own teacher used to point out that she did not set out to build a big monastery when she came to this country. She was quite surprised to see it grow the way it did. But I well remember that no matter how small we were, she never let us behave as if we were anything less than a Dai Hon Zan, or "Great Dharma Temple." The ceremony hall, or "Hondo," was never too small to do the ceremonies completely, even if we were squirming around on a postage stamp. Her aspiration was to give us the best she knew how to give, and never to shortchange us; nor let us shortchange ourselves. It was because of this that the monastery grew the way it did, until one day we had a Hondo to match this aspiration. It was just such aspiration that gave all the ancient masters the strength to spread the Dharma, so that today it has reached all four quarters of the globe. There is not one shred of ego ambition in this. I pray that I will partake of this same aspiration, so that this Temple may prosper too. I have a strong desire to see it become everything that it can become, and I especially wish to see the lay Sangha develop depth of practice and to grow in wisdom.

Lay life is full of opportunities to develop this practice and cultivate wisdom. First, recognize within yourself the Mind that seeks the Way. This is the pure aspiration to seek the Truth. It is what brought you to study Zen in the first place. Next, remind yourself of it every day, do your meditation, and study the Precepts. Focus carefully on every action, and soon your deepest aspiration will permeate each moment. Then, don't give up. Keep at this practice, redoubling your efforts when you feel yourself flagging. In time this aspiration will define your very life, and the deepest Truth will be yours. There is a story from *Zen Flesh, Zen Bones* that illustrates this perfectly.

> A young physician in Tokyo named Kusuda met a college friend who had been studying Zen. The young doctor asked him what Zen was.
>
> "I cannot tell you what it is," the friend replied, "but one thing is certain. If you understand Zen, you will not be afraid to die."
>
> "That's fine, said Kusuda. "I will try it. Where can I find a teacher?"
>
> "Go to the master Nanin," the friend told him.
>
> So Kusuda went to call on Nanin. He carried a dagger nine and a half inches long to determine whether or not the teacher himself was afraid to die.

When Nanin saw Kusuda, he exclaimed: "Hello, friend. How are you? We haven't seen each other for a long time!"

This perplexed Kusuda, who replied: "We have never met before." "That's right," answered Nanin. "I mistook you for another physician who is receiving instruction here."

With such a beginning, Kusuda lost his chance to test the master, so reluctantly he asked if he might receive Zen instruction.

Nanin said: "Zen is not a difficult task. If you are a physician, treat your patients with kindness. That is Zen."

Kusuda visited Nanin three times. Each time Nanin told him the same thing. "A physician should not waste time around here. Go home and take care of your patients."

It was not yet clear to Kusuda how such teaching could remove the fear of death. So on his fourth visit he complained: "My friend told me that when one learns Zen one loses his fear of death. Each time I come here all you tell me is to take care of my patients. I know that much. If that is your so-called Zen, I am not going to visit you any more."

Nanin smiled and patted the doctor. "I have been too strict with you. Let me give you a koan." He presented Kusuda with Joshu's Mu to work over, which is the first mind-enlightening problem in the book called *The Gateless Gate*.

Kusuda pondered this problem of Mu (No-Thing) for two years. At length he thought he had reached certainty of mind. But his teacher commented: "You are not in yet."

Kusuda continued in concentration for another year and a half. His mind became placid. Problems dissolved. No-Thing became the truth. He served his patients well and, without even knowing it, he was free from concern over life and death.

Then when he visited Nanin, his old teacher just smiled.[4]

The Measure of Perfection

Shuzan held out his short staff and said:

> If you call this a short staff, you oppose its reality. If you do not
> call it a short staff, you ignore the fact. Now what do you wish
> to call this?

When my teacher commented on this story, she quoted another
teacher who summed up all he had learned after a long life of Zen
practice, saying, "One stick is as long as it is; one stick is as short as
it is." In Japan there is a variety of radish called a daikon, which
means "big root," because it gets to be quite big. My master's master
was small, even for a Japanese man of his generation. One of his
favorite sayings was:

> A daikon is still a daikon, even when it is small.

An object either is a stick or a radish, or it isn't. Since size has
nothing to do with it, qualities like stickness or radishness are not
subject to measurement or comparison. It can be very helpful to
remember this, particularly when considering matters pertaining to
the deepest Truth.

There was a monk from England in training at the monastery when
I was there. She had learned about meditation and Zen practice at a
temple over there, and like many people, she went through an early
period of great enthusiasm. About that time she took a job at a
nursing care facility for people recovering from severe injuries, many
of whom were paralyzed. She realized later that in the back of her
mind was the thought that the positivity and centeredness she was
finding through practice would somehow benefit patients going through
tough times. Instead of opening up to her positivity, however, the
patients were surly and unresponsive, giving her the message to bug
off. One day a man came to visit the facility. He was a quadriplegic
and was confined to a wheelchair. He had already been through the
very same pain and anguish those patients were experiencing right
then, and he came to talk to them about finding the heart to go on in
the midst of it. My friend will swear that when he first entered the

room, it became lighter in there. He spoke to each person, radiating warmth, and each was touched in some way. The mood in the hospital remained warmer and brighter for days. My friend realized that this severely disabled man, through his own positivity, grace, and certainty, was much better equipped to help other handicapped people than she was. Trying to give them aid and comfort, she herself was handicapped by the fact that she did not have the same experiences as those she was helping.

The difference between my friend and the quadriplegic, however, is much more a matter of perception than of Truth. The measure of perfection does not attach to any condition. We are all relatively strong in some ways, relatively weak in others. "Whole," or "perfect," as we usually understand the terms with respect to human existence, really means falling within average parameters. Yet it is very easy to imagine living in a world where people live hundreds of years, are vastly more intelligent than we are now, and are taller, stronger, more agile, faster, healthier, and so on. In such a world, people as we are today would be hopelessly handicapped. Does that make us less able to touch the very deepest Truth—to *know* enlightenment itself? Absolutely not. *Expressions* of wisdom may depend on differing capabilities, but despite differences with regard to mental or physical qualities, we are one within the Buddha Mind. One stick is as long as it is; one stick is as short as it is. So put away your tape measures; both are sticks, perfect, just as they are.

This matter of mental and physical health and its relationship to spiritual practice has been fraught with much confusion. The realm of body and mind may be subject to measurement and comparison, but, ultimately, enlightenment is not. First of all, the things we do and the choices we make have consequences, and this operates in both the spiritual and physical dimensions. Therefore, as we develop in spiritual discipline, clean up our karma, and live more wholesome lives, tremendous changes can take place in our mental and physical well-being. When we don't want to face the consequences of our actions on the physical level, and avoid making the changes necessary for good health, we are not being responsible for our own bodies, which my teacher always said was a primary Buddhist duty. In addition, we are compounding ignorance. However, we put the cart before the horse when we measure health, diet, lifestyle, etc., and give them spiritual labels. Fundamentally, it is not spiritually more profound to be healthy, live long, avoid stress, or eat purely. In fact, some very worthy choices come at some cost to health. Self-sacrifice, even of life itself, can be undergone for the sake of others, to achieve something noble in life, or for the Truth itself. Such self-sacrifice is at the core of a Bodhisattva act. A very simple example of this is a choice I faced sometimes when driving late at night. Too much caffeine can give me a headache. But occasionally I would be asked by my teacher to drive her to a distant destination late at night. When tired, I would drink a big cup of coffee thinking better a headache tomorrow than an accident tonight. This was not a major act of self-sacrifice on my part, but it illustrates the point that you cannot measure training by a yardstick of purity, health, or lifestyle. To put it another way, these things may arise as a result of practice, but practice is not dependent upon these things.

It is said that Bodhisattvas give up enjoying their own enlightenment for the sake of all living things. It is because we live in the world and have many responsibilities that this is so. I gained a tremendous insight into this by watching the veterinarian who treated our goats at the monastery. He worked tirelessly for their benefit yet could exhibit astonishing insensitivity to their suffering. I realized that he, like most medical people, I presume, had to be insensitive to some degree in order to handle his job at all. To achieve a greater good, he sacrificed something of himself. Hopefully, over time, he has been able to reopen himself to the sensitivity he had to protect. This principle applies to all of us, however. As parents, priests, working people, what-have-you, we give up some of our peace and quiet and complicate our lives in order to give of ourselves. Not to do so is to fail to participate in the functioning of enlightenment itself. I think it is important to remember this when we consider matters like health, well-being, and peace of mind.

There are many people who say that Zen has nothing to do with such things as health and healing. But zazen attaches itself to nothing, nor does it reject anything. All things are possible in this world, especially when we do not reject them out of hand but rather allow things to manifest naturally. I also run into many people who are looking to escape the consequences of being born as a mortal human being. To them I answer that looking for a triumph over eventual physical decay and death misses the fundamental point of Buddhism. For myself, I see a vital intersection between spiritual practice and the development of a healthy body and mind. I would like to borrow from the Hindu tradition to paint a picture. Please understand that I am not trying to explain Hinduism; I am simply borrowing from it to make this illustration.

The Hindu term for the Cosmic Buddha, or absolute Godhead, is Brahman. Brahman is absolutely everything yet exceeds all creation by one span. He is total unity and perfection and more. He appears in three primary aspects: Brahma,* the Creator; Shiva, the Destroyer; and Vishnu, the Preserver. When I was in my early teens, my biggest religious problem could have been summed up in a rather silly question: "What possible purpose can things like flies and mosquitoes that spread disease, and the bacteria and viruses that cause disease, possibly have in a world in which everything is supposedly created for some good?" Back then I understood the standard explanation of the cycle of life; i.e. cows eat grass and in turn fertilize the ground, etc. I knew that the more life exists in any particular place, the richer it becomes. I knew that insects help the life cycle by pollinating plants, and so forth, but what good were flies and mosquitoes? It struck me one day that the whole process is a cycle not just of becoming, but also of deterioration, which in itself is another form of becoming. Bacteria digest the grass in the cow's stomach, and other bacteria break down the fecal matter so that it can be taken as nutrients by more plants. In the same way, plants that die become mulch for richer soil and future vegetation. The problem with the question I was asking was in the fact that I was placing myself, as a member of humanity, at the center of the universe. I wanted to know, "What good are flies, mosquitoes, bacteria, and viruses to *me*?" This question arose in the context of my Christian upbringing. In the Bible it says

---

*Hindu terminology uses the term "Brahma" for the creator as distinguished from "Brahman," the Godhead; however Buddhist scriptures, when referring to this same concept, often use the name "Indra" for the creative force.

that God gave humanity dominion over the earth and everything that creeps and crawls, swims and flies thereon. I discovered this means that we have a responsibility to take care of this earth and its many creatures by learning the true meaning of compassion, and not that all creation is subject to our will, nor that we are free from the natural cycle of creation and deterioraion. As a carrier of disease, then, the humble mosquito is an agent of Shiva, and mighty human beings are subject to the lowly virus. It is easy to see the perfection of this cycle in the decomposition of grass and fecal matter; it is another to recognize it in one's own mortality. To do this requires dropping egocentric, even specio-centric, attachment.

So birth, growth, sprouting, budding, and blooming are all aspects of Brahma, the Creator, while old age, disease, death, and decay are aspects of Shiva, the Destroyer. It took me many more years to understand Vishnu, the Preserver, however, and it wasn't until I had been a Buddhist monk for some time that I began to understand his function. I discovered that he represents a balance between the other two. Turning to the spiritual side of this in our own meditation practice, clinging or attachment would be an excess of Brahma, while rejecting or avoidance would be an excess of Shiva. Vishnu, the Preserver, would represent the balance of neither rejecting nor clinging, allowing things to come and go in their own natural time. We can see this principle of preservation through balance in the external world, in that overpopulation in any species leads to disease or starvation. This is just one way in which Brahma and Shiva can be out of balance, and then famine, pestilence, and disease bring about untimely death. But when they are in balance, which is the function of Vishnu, by and large things come and go in their own natural time, and so Vishnu is called the Preserver.

At every moment we are each changing mentally, physically, and spiritually. It is said that we renew our bodies every seven years, because at each moment some cells are dying while others take their place. Creation and dissolution, birth and death, are occurring simultaneously each moment. But as it is physically, so it is mentally and spiritually. Rebirth is exactly this process on all levels. Our emotional and mental makeup changes over the years and develops well or poorly depending upon how we train ourselves. In meditation we develop a healthy spirit by allowing thoughts, emotions, greeds, hates, delusions, samadhis, and enlightenment experiences to come and go in their own natural way. Just as a healthy body that is neither too heavy nor too light depends in part upon the right balance of rest, food, and exercise, so Zen training and the balance it brings leads to a healthy spirit. Now it is well known that body, mind, and spirit are not separate things. It is known that bad diet can lead to mental aberrations and spiritual problems. But the causal links work the other way as well. Some doctors now believe that many diseases have essentially spiritual causes. Although medical science has been able to discover a great deal about the physical processes of disease, it is more difficult to determine why some people get them and others do not. With regard to this, some doctors are beginning to suspect that spiritual factors are sometimes more important than physical ones in determining susceptibility to disease.

This is a very complex matter, and it would be stupid to conclude too quickly that an illness or untimely death is due to negative spiritual factors. For one thing, it sometimes happens that when someone begins or deepens her practice and makes a change in her life, she sets up the circumstances for karmic consequence catching up with her. Also, the karma of being born as a human being of this or that race and sex, that one is only so tall, so intelligent, and so strong, is the karma of this life and cannot be commuted. But while frailty and death are inherent in birth, this does not stand against perfection. Real perfection is not subject to measurement and calculation, just as the deepest Truth cannot be proved or disproved by facts and reason. Even so, it is still true that our internal spiritual state is a very important factor with regard to our health. As many teachers have pointed out, our actions and habits of body and mind can place strains on us that can lead to disease. Meditation and genuine training can cure these tendencies. Meditation, in that it leads to balance and cleaning up our lives, acts as Vishnu, the Preserver, and helps each of us to live according to our own natural span of years, whatever that may be, and this is the healing power of Zen. The ultimate purpose of Zen, however, is the realization of the deepest Truth, or we could say, coming to know the Cosmic Buddha. In this analogy, that would be Brahman. So Zen does not focus on Vishnu as Preserver *per se*, because the eternal life of Zen is not one of eternal self-preservation, but that of eternal Brahman, of which we are a part. Vishnu is one aspect of Brahman, and as balance, he represents our practice of meditation and daily training. If we really train ourselves hard, looking beyond the superficial appearances of things, rejecting nothing as impossible, we can learn a great deal about how karma works. In the process we stop perpetuating the imbalance between becoming and dissolving that stands in the way of enlightenment and health as well.

Some people regard healing as miraculous. I would not argue with that. Life itself is miraculous. Others deny the miraculous, but that's often an expression of a closed mind. While I have seen things I cannot explain, to me the miraculous is the occurrence of some natural process the observer does not yet understand. So the realm of the possible will always be greater for those whose minds are not closed by skepticism. An open mind doesn't mean we must believe everything we're told, just not reject things out of hand. Actually, I think that not being open to the myriad possibilities in life is a major obstacle to understanding. All things teach and enlighten us if we look at life with the eye of meditation and recognize that nothing is outside the realm of the Buddha. To become preoccupied with matters of health and well-being is to miss the point of Zen, but to rationalize, psychologize, or limit it is a very shallow view indeed.

Drifting Clouds, Flowing Water

"Here's a question for you. How can I manage to practice nonattachment when everything I have is invested in this business? In this situation, everything I have worked for, and that others have worked for too, could be lost tomorrow. Just one false move and we'd all be out of work." I was being asked, in effect, "How can I be responsible in a really tough situation like this if I remain unattached, and don't care about how things turn out?" The man asking this question was one who had had a career working for government agencies and was in the process of starting his own company. It was at that critical, fledgling stage of beginning to take off, but in need of constant care and feeding. The pressures on him were tremendous and unrelenting, for one miscalculation and his savings and life's work could be lost, and that of others as well. But in terms of practice, he was far from alone in this predicament. The specifics of his situation may have been different, but this question is the same one asked by Buddhists for centuries. It has always been the case that responsible people, at home as well as at work, find that others depend upon them, sometimes a great deal. It can seem that every way they turn there are commitments and responsibilities. In addition, this man was at an age when he could see the many options of youth dropping away. As we recognize this happening, it becomes clear how the choices we make can have profound, long-term consequences. Therefore, they require very careful consideration. What does nonattachment mean in these situations? And how in the world does nonattachment harmonize with the idea of commitment?

The word for a Buddhist monk in Sino-Japanese is "Unsui," literally "cloud, water." It comes, originally, from the phrase "gyoun-ryusyu," or "drifting clouds, flowing water."[6] Neither clouds nor water insist upon any particular form, for they take shape according to conditions. Clouds attach to nothing, and so drift freely across the sky. Water twists and turns on its way down hill in complete accord with the path it must follow. The flowing of the water has the strength to move mountains, while the drifting of the clouds is utterly free. In these qualities we have a perfect description of the Zen mind. Just as clouds cling to nothing, floating free and changing with the wind, acceptance of change is the essence of nonattachment and expresses the perfect freedom of meditation. Flowing water follows its course naturally, without resistance or hesitation. This lack of resistance describes the *willingness* at the heart of a true commitment to Zen practice, which like water, has the strength to move mountains. To become a monk, an Unsui, requires ordination. By its very nature, ordination means a deep commitment to the form of practice we call Zen Buddhism. It also means a commitment to a teacher, and to a Sangha, or community of fellow trainees. Ordination means a commitment to a life of training in nonattachment, so right from the very beginning, the concepts of nonattachment and commitment are present together in Zen teaching.

What exactly does nonattachment in Zen practice mean? First of all, it does not imply a lack of feeling, or a quietistic unconcern. Basically, nonattachment means all-acceptance with willingness and positivity of mind. All-acceptance means complete willingness to admit that things are exactly as they are. This implies absolutely nothing about whether or not they can or should be changed, but it does mean seeing things clearly. After all, we can't understand something that is right in front of us if we do not first accept that it is. When we see things clearly with an all-accepting mind, we stand a much better chance of acting wisely. All-acceptance means to drop the "self," with all its preferences, opinions, and attachments, whenever it arises, remembering our own free, natural mind of meditation.

In the practice of all-acceptance, one of the toughest things to do is to drop attachment to the results of our most carefully planned actions. Because we usually have strong expectations about how our efforts should turn out, we often can't accept the results we actually get. Wisdom will be quickly lost, despite our good intentions, if we are unable to live in nonattachment while in the midst of endeavors we care very much about. Nonattachment does not, therefore, mean we can indulge in the selfish "freedom" of dropping responsibility, but rather that we make a vow to drop self-centeredness in the midst of responsible action.

Now what about commitment? Commitment, of course, always implies taking on responsibility. If "resolve" is the effort we bring forth at each moment, commitment is the willingness to keep at something over time. Commitment in Zen practice means to try to do our best in all situations to make our lives an expression of that practice. A job, marriage, family ties, relationship to a temple, as well as becoming a monk, can all be expressions of practice if we make a commitment to ourselves to make it so. Commitment means a willingness to be relied upon, time and time again, in specific ways. As a parent, spouse, or friend it is in sharing ourselves with others, as in giving *and* receiving emotional and physical support. As a worker, it is in giving our best effort and being part of the team. As a man or woman on the path of Zen, it is in making all actions expressions of that practice. You can make the whole world your monastery, and all living things your Sangha if you are sincere in this. It is through this practice that we come to see the Truth appearing everywhere. Whether or not those around us also practice does not matter if we concentrate hard on making our own lives expressions of practice. It can be done, but it takes real commitment to do it.

While it is true that living and practicing as a monk are different than lay life and practice, some things are not so different as many people think. The entrepreneur with his life savings at stake has no more invested in his enterprise than a monk does in his practice. Some years ago, while still living at the monastery, I faced knee surgery. This was no great matter medically, but with it came the realization that I had no financial resources whatsoever of my own. The monastery could not help me, and I found that I had to seek public assistance. I was just about 30 years old at the time, and I had spent the previous eight years in the monastery. I had worked very hard and learned a great deal, but my rewards were not in the least bit financial. It was then that it occurred to me that with each passing year doors were closing behind me. I realized with great clarity that it is very difficult to consider another career when just about your entire work experience is as a Zen monk. Not that I would ever want to, fortunately, but the seriousness of the decision I made in my early 20's became vividly clear. A monk invests his life in developing selflessness, and he forgoes other things. Yet, in a very real sense, he is just as tied to this commitment, if not more so, as a layman is to his career and family. The true freedom of the Unsui, it turns out, is realized when he fully embraces the depth of commitment the life demands, willingly following the course of training without resistance, like flowing water. It is definitely not found in a "carefree" nonattachment. It is in this commitment to selflessness that the deepest meaning of Zen training is found, and it is in commitment that the practice of nonattachment has its deepest form.

Nonattachment and commitment meet in willingness. The willingness to accept things as they are, and the willingness to let things go; *this* is the essence of nonattachment. The willingness to give of ourselves, to be depended upon, and the willingness to keep at a form of practice over time; *this* is the essence of commitment. Willingness is the mind bright and positive, the will flexible, the ability to bow; what could better sum up Zen practice?

Zen training is sometimes referred to as stillness within activity, and activity within stillness. In compassionate all-acceptance we find the life of Kanzeon Bosatsu:* stillness, the quiet of meditation, the essence of nonattachment. In responsibility we find the life of Fugen Bosatsu: loving action, transcendence of the opposites, the true meaning of commitment. Stillness and activity, nonattachment and commitment, are the clouds and water of the Unsui. Together they lead to the life of Monju, wisdom itself. A life of nonattachment without commitment is like a tree without its roots in the ground. It will grow progressively weaker, so how could this be true freedom? Nonattachment within commitment brings peace of mind when you know that you can bow no matter how things turn out, even should your business fail; for then you can know that you have done your very best. In the life of a Zen trainee, success at the deepest level is found in this willingness to accept all things positively, the willingness to bow, and it is not measured by any external yardstick. You can make your own

---

*The three Bodhisattvas of Kanzeon, Fugen, and Monju (Avalokitesvara, Samantabhadra, and Manjusri in Sanskrit), represent the Buddha's compassion, loving kindness, and wisdom, respectively. They are three aspects of enlightenment that exist within each of us.

life an expression of this practice by embracing your many responsibilities within nonattachment. The duties of daily life can be transformed into a commitment to practice if you vow to perform them
compassionately and with all-acceptance, drop attachment to results,
and vow to keep going each day and to do your best for all concerned. This requires the willingness to accept things as they are, and
the willingness to be depended upon. It requires keeping the mind
bright and positive, the will flexible, and the ability to bow; what
could better sum up Zen training?

GOD USES THE GOOD ONES

In the 1971 movie *Parade of Fools*, Jimmy Stewart plays a man who is released from prison in 1935, at the height of the Great Depression. While in prison he had managed to save $25,000, bit by bit, participating in a convict work program. He and two other released convicts decide to start a general store in another state. Unfortunately, a corrupt bank official has been misappropriating the work program funds given to the bank to manage. The official quickly realizes that covering a $25,000 check would expose the shortage of funds and his own wrong doing. He turns to a religious fanatic bent on punishing sinners, and lining his own pockets on the side. This man has a pair of lunatic sidekicks, one of whom likes to hear atheists repent just before he shoots them. The bank official turns this lot loose on the convicts to do them in before they can collect their funds. After many adventures that nearly get them killed, our heroes realize that the first religious fanatic has done in the others to keep the money for himself. One of Jimmy Stewart's buddies says of the killer, "It's kind of queer, him being a Sunday School teacher and all." Stewart's character replies, "Well, I guess God uses the good ones. But the bad ones, they use God."

Years ago, when Gyokuko and I moved to Eugene to take on the Temple there, we found that it was almost unknown in the community since there had been no resident priest, and virtually no regular public events for ages. So we placed some listings in local directories and ran an ad in a local "take one" style newspaper. The publicity did a lot of good, for it put the Temple back on the map and got things going again. But it also drew the attention of some people who were less than pleased that a Buddhist group was active in the area. Pretty soon we began to receive inquiries from people, mostly younger males, who would begin by asking about our practice. Eventually they would come around to a question like, "Well, do you worship Buddha?" or "Did Buddha die for your sins?" No matter what the answer, it would lead to the payoff, "Do you know that you are going to Hell?"

It didn't take very long to get good at recognizing these phone calls early in the opening "inquiry" stage, but unfortunately the nature of the calls changed quickly. In a month or two, they became openly harassing and taunting and would sometimes come in the middle of the night. Although just hanging up works the best, most of the time the caller would hang up himself when asked for his name or other information. One day a young man and his friend called, asked the usual questions, then quickly became very snide and insulting. When I asked for their names, they hung up, then called right back. They gave their names and reported they had been told about the Temple in their Sunday School class. They gave the name of their teacher and the gist of what he had to say. I was amazed, and thought of contacting the man just to let him know what had happened. But after some discrete inquiries, I realized it would only add fuel to the fire. Right about this time, we also had difficulties with people removing our retreat posters, with impressive efficiency, from notice boards on a nearby college campus. As you can imagine, this did not incline me toward generous thoughts when it came to certain brands of Christianity.

One day I took a phone call from a man who began by making tentative inquiries about who we were and what we did. I was immediately on my guard. When I had cautiously explained who we were, he announced that he was an instructor at an evangelical college in the state. "Oh boy", I thought, "Where are we headed now?" Then he totally floored me by admitting that he was always nervous when calling a group like ours. He often found strong negative feelings in these groups, generated by bad experiences with other conservative Christians. "We're not all like that, you know," he said in a deeply apologetic way. Talk about unexpected! I confess I stammered a bit. He went on to tell me that he liked to expose his students to other religious points of view but always felt he had to poke his hat in through the door on a stick to see if it was safe. As he spoke, I recognized in what he had to say elements of recent experiences of my own. This was at a time when Oregon had just experienced public friction with Scientologists, Hare Krishna groups, and others and was just entering the height of its conflict with the Rajneeshies. Gyokuko and I had to make it a rule never to step out the door in our robes. It didn't seem to matter that we weren't all the same; all unfamiliar religious groups, particularly eastern religious groups, were lumped together in popular conception. Even that most general and innocuous of topics that begins, "Oh, and what do you do for a living?" which comes up in the barber's chair, doctor's office, or standing in a grocery line, could lead to a very strained situation. We found it wiser to slip around those questions if we could. So there he was, an Evangelical Christian, describing to me a problem I knew myself so very well. We compared notes. It is hard to explain how comforting I found it.

It is said in Zen that enlightened action leaves no wake. That means that when we go about our daily lives mindfully, living carefully and minding our own business, we don't make a lot of noise or kick up a lot of dust. An enlightened daily life is an unexciting thing. To most people it is virtually invisible. One conclusion my Evangelical friend and I came to was that from now on we would remember each other. So now, whenever I run into difficulties with a Christian fanatic, I will remember him. After all, in many ways it is he and other quiet Christians who are hurt by such actions, not I. Scandal rocks every type of organized human group, so the next time he hears of a scandal plaguing an organization following an eastern path, he has agreed to remember that there are many people on that path who raise no dust and go unnoticed. I think remembering this would help in other arenas where there is conflict: between Arabs and Jews; blacks and whites; men and women; Bosnians and Serbs. It's so easy to notice only those that offend against our own interests.

These days it seems that every group has its turn under public scrutiny for the highly visible actions of a few. Some paths may be deep, some not so deep; some may emphasize self-sacrifice, while others have a joyful message; it really doesn't matter. Those who take a path sincerely and quietly will largely go unnoticed. Those who make a mess of it will stand out in the glaring light of publicity. A religious practice may be good for some, and not so good for others; it will have its strong points and its weak points. But it does little good to judge a whole tradition by the glaring faults of those who use God's name for their own ends, for in all traditions the quiet ones go about their lives unnoticed, being used by God.

SUPERSTITION

Once upon a time there was a woman who had a set of six very beautiful cups. In her kitchen, right over the spot where she kept her tea pot, there was a handy little shelf that was almost perfect for storing her cups. Unfortunately, the shelf was really only big enough to hold five of them. However, she found that if she arranged them very carefully, she could just squeeze all six cups together in a tight little row. One evening, while in a rush to get to a meeting, she dried her good cups and put them away. Her children had been making a fuss all evening, and now one of them was at her again, tugging at her skirt as she put the last cup on the shelf. "What is it now?" she asked, looking down at the little girl as she worked. As soon as she let go of the cup, she knew what was going to happen. She felt it slip away from her hand, and "Crash!" it hit the counter and scattered hopelessly into little bits of chips and shards. "Now look what you made me do!" she yelled at the little girl standing there at her feet.

Superstition is a word linked to all kinds of things, but something that lies at the base of all superstitious behavior is a blurring of causal relationships. I once read that researchers found that they could induce "superstitious" behavior in rats by first teaching them to pull a lever to get food. Then they would proceed to disassociate the reward from the pulling of the lever; first by giving a reward of food every other time, then with a probability of one time in three, and then, say, twice in seven or eight times. They found that as the connection between lever-pulling and reward became more random, the rat would become much more involved in trying to "win" the reward, spending more and more time pulling the lever than she ever had before. Then she would begin to exhibit "superstitious" behavior. She might repeat certain movements, for example, such as running back and forth or turning around in a circle, that had happened once to coincide with gaining a reward. This, they observed, was different from other learning behavior in that it only had to "work" once for the rat to repeat it many times. There is an exact parallel here to the things that gamblers and sports figures often do. They wear the same shirt, carry lucky objects, or perform elaborate rituals before a game because somehow those things have become associated with the desired reward. The funny thing is, we so often do something very similar in our everyday lives in the way we praise or blame other people, things, or ourselves for the way events turn out. When someone blames short-term causes for his long-term problems, it is not that different from believing a lucky shirt can help him win at poker. The woman with six cups set up the probability of breaking one when she decided to store them on a shelf only big enough for five. It was really just a matter of time before something distracted her enough to "cause" her to break a cup. It was just by chance that she was in a rush to get to that *particular* meeting, and it was just by chance that her daughter happened to call to her at the moment she did. Yet you can imagine the things that went through her mind about why that cup got broken.

Despite our strong belief that ours is a heritage of scientific objectivity, there are many ways in which we born to western culture tend to blur causal connections. Many western Buddhists claim that they do not believe that there is an arbitrary force at work in the universe that affects the world in order to bring about reward and punishment for our behavior. Yet they will often believe, for example, the axiom that "Pride comes before a fall" in a way that implies exactly that. Rather than "pride", it is usually "carelessness" that comes before a fall. But pride, in turn, often leads to carelessness. Sometimes pride sets up haughty behavior, spawning the ill will of others, or leads to taking on more than can be handled, etc., and any of these can then bring about the "fall." While most people readily understand these causal routes, many still, at the same time, enjoy the thought that there is some intervening hand that willfully plays a part in this.

Everyone remembers the ocean liner *Titanic*, which so tragically sank in the North Atlantic. It was back in the headlines and on people's minds when the wreck was discovered in the mid-eighties, and attempts to salvage items from it began. Few situations illustrate more perfectly this point about blurring causal relationships than the story of the Titanic. During the salvage operations the story was often repeated, emphasizing the claim of "unsinkability," which arrogantly "tempted fate." Inherent in the very language of such stories is the implication that there was some sort of willful being out there that was offended by such arrogance, so sent the iceberg in retribution. In hearing the story retold, it is clear that many people believe that the arrogance of the ship owners actually caused the iceberg to appear. I agree that as a poetic symbol it is powerful and very apt. But to take it literally is not the Buddhist point of view.

The arrogance of the ship owners lead to overconfidence and a terrible lack of preparation. Those things lead to the tragic loss of life, and so it can be said that arrogance caused the tragedy. Maybe it even affected the way the ship was handled, so that an opportunity to avoid the collision was lost. But there was no causal link between the arrogance and the fact that the iceberg occupied the position it did when the collision occurred. Probabilities and natural law will work most of the same consequences as any willful "hand of retribution," and without any implication of petty human motivation like vengeance, anger, or pique.

People often say to themselves, "I must be doing something right," or, "Somebody up there likes me," when things unexpectedly work out. But the flip side of that attitude is "Why me? What did I do to deserve this?" A tornado once tore through a town and flattened the houses on both sides of a third house left untouched. While one family deeply and sincerely offered prayers of gratitude to God for their deliverance, their neighbors found themselves in quite a quandary. One man realized that deep inside he was very angry at God for singling him out, which was a feeling he was not equipped to handle. Meanwhile, the other neighbor found that, in spite of herself, she couldn't help searching her soul, looking for the sin that "caused" such a terrible retribution. Watching other peoples' problems from a safe distance, we think how silly such thoughts are. But the tendency to look at life just that way is very strong indeed. How do you make sense of an event like that?

To look at the world with Buddhist eyes is to gaze at the mystery of life with a sense of wonder. Careful consideration of cause and effect does not diminish this one bit. A deep and meaningful feeling arises as we become aware of the significance of events; the cycle of life, death, and change. When the "hand of fate" picks my house to be flattened by a tornado, I choose the dilemma of wondering "Why me?" when I compare my fate to my neighbor's. But if I choose to accept that when pain comes there is pain, and when joy comes there is joy, I am one step closer to knowing that I am always bound together with all life, all events, all *things* in the great ocean of Truth. This is the well-spring of gratitude in Buddhism. It is also the source of humility in Buddhism.

Looking at the law of cause and effect on a more internal level, we can consider our own tendencies to things like anger, fear, depression, or frustration. Certain things may happen to us in the course of a day that set off these feelings. The feelings themselves may be perfectly natural, or they may be due to karmic conditioning. In either case, the events themselves do not *make* us get angry, afraid, depressed, or frustrated. Yet we tend to hold an image in our minds of the things themselves as having the power to make us angry or afraid. When these things are genuinely unhealthy, or even just short-term contributors to negative states of mind, it is sometimes good to avoid them when possible. However, it is said in Buddhism that to taste enlightenment we must overcome the obstacle of suffering we have inherited. To do this we need to turn our attention inward to understand the predispositions we have within ourselves to habitually react in the ways we do, for that is where we come face-to-face with our own obstacles to enlightenment. Examining causal relationships can aid us in understanding and overcoming those obstacles, but not if we confuse ourselves with superstitious views. The workings of life are mysterious and wonderful. We *should* look upon them with awe and reverence. But it does not further reverence to be confused concerning causal relationships. Instead, look at life carefully, consider why things happen, and turn this careful attention inward to find peace of mind, gratitude, and true reverence.

SINGLE ENLIGHTENMENT
& THE PROMISE OF SPRING

One day some years ago, Gyokuko and I were walking together on a particularly beautiful morning in May. The sun was bright and warm, while the air was refreshingly cool. The azaleas and rhododendrons were spectacular, and every so often we noticed something sweet and fragrant filling the air. It had been a long winter, wet and cold, and that morning brought the first real warming of the year. With the warmth of the sun on my face, and the flowers in bright light, it was finally possible to believe in my bones that summer could actually come again.

Have you ever noticed that in midwinter, picking up a coat when you go outside for a walk is automatic, but it is almost impossible to imagine a hot day, when all you want to wear is shorts and a T-shirt? The sensations of a season can become part of your consciousness, so that the feel of a winter day years ago seems closer somehow, and easier to recall, than the way things felt last summer. Then, on the first really hot day of the year, you might notice little things like the feel of a hot car seat, or being slightly sticky with sweat, or the constant presence of insects, and awareness of them seems to come back like long-lost memories. In *Uji*, Dogen says that the past, present, and future flow into one another.[7] On our walk that beautiful morning in spring, similar days long ago, with the heady scent of jasmine where I grew up, flowed into the present, and I had a strong feeling for what Dogen meant. But there was something else, too. That spring day held the promise that winter would end, and a long, warm summer would come. It is because we have experienced summer many times before that we are able to feel its potential on a day in spring. Every moment holds a promise, the potential for things as yet unseen. It is because we learn from past experience that we are able to feel the promise that exists in whatever we find before us.

A very young child lives entirely within the present moment, as do animals. They are completely at one with what they experience, but in a way that is called in Buddhism "single enlightenment."[8] This level of awareness does not yet touch the potential beyond the immediate moment, nor does it include deep empathy for, nor understanding of, the experiences of others. A cat curled up and purring on your lap is completely at one with you at that moment. He is aware of you as part of his world, and he may be able to sense subtle changes in your state of mind. But he is not aware of you as a separate being with your own needs and a world view that is as valid as his own. This is why he may, in his contentment, rhythmically work his claws into your leg. You are, to him, wonderfully accommodating furniture. In the same way, an infant cries when she is hungry without a thought for whether feeding her at that moment is convenient for her mother. She is aware only that she is hungry. As children get older, they become increasingly aware that other people, and other forces in the world, operate independently of their own desires. This is often painful, but it leads to an understanding that there is a difference between "self" and "other." If there is a point to Zen training, it is to harmonize the all-is-one with the all-is-different. As we do this, the ability to truly empathize with others develops. It's wonderful to realize that we can't empathize with others until we can see that they are different from us. Then we can begin to understand them as they really are, instead of just projecting our own experiences onto them. To get to this point, we have to know that we do not sit at the center of the universe. Within single enlightenment, a child lives entirely within the present moment, but in a rather selfish and limited way. When a child is happy, he knows only that he is happy—deliriously happy. When he is sad, he knows nothing other than sadness. The same is true for pain, fear, or any other feeling. For him, at each moment, no other reality can exist. Because of this, a very young child has no patience and no comprehension of what will come, for he has as yet little past experience. On a warm spring day he may be fully in the moment, but he will not yet feel the promise held within it.

Adults, very often, are too involved in what was, or in what may be, so that they loose their centeredness, which only exists in the present. They need to rediscover their childlike wonder within the moment. But to do so while remaining aware of past experience, and while retaining an understanding of causality, is to be able to taste the promise of spring *within* the moment. This requires the kind of naiveté that arises from simplicity of mind but is not childish or foolish at all. In fact, this naiveté is a necessary element in real wisdom. Zen practice does not aim for a regression to childlike single enlightenment, but rather to harmonizing the all-is-one with the all-is-different. This requires being ourselves completely, and then understanding our own limitations, karma, past suffering, strengths, and foibles, and yet getting beyond them to touch something fundamental. It is only when we do this that we are able to completely empathize with others, for then we can accept their limitations, karma, strengths, and foibles also and understand that they do not stand against our oneness with them in the deepest and most fundamental place.

In Zen practice we should grow up and be adults, fully and completely. The secret, though, is to harmonize our childlike naiveté and wonder with adult maturity and discernment. The way to peace of mind and to enlightenment is always forward. Be very careful of paths and teachers that advocate a return to a childlike, carefree life, abandoning responsibilities, and completely giving up one's own judgement. This is not a path back to Eden, but to dependency and loss of autonomy. We can't go back to Eden, but this is no great loss. The path of Buddhist training is always forward, for that is where our lives are. Always going forward, going on, we find that Nirvana is right here.

MOZART, BUDDHIST CHANTS & CONSCIOUSNESS

One spring evening I had the pleasure of attending a Portland Symphony concert with Ani Paldrön, a Tibetan nun and head of the Portland Sakya Center. The program included Mozart's *Mass in C Major (The Great)*, plus some extracts from Wagner's *Götterdämmerung*, Siegfried's *Rhine Journey* and *Funeral March*, plus the *Immolation of Brunhilde*. It was quite an entertaining selection, so I was looking forward to a wonderful evening.

I really love Mozart. He had an incredible sense of melody, with beautiful structure and development. While I sat listening to the *Mass*, however, I was struck by how "self-conscious" it seemed. I don't mean the work is self-conscious in an awkward or clumsy way. It's just that the whole composition is very carefully planned, developed, and constructed in a manner that is quite deliberate, and therefore, *conscious*. Nonetheless, there were times when the music was so absorbing that it swept away awareness of time and place, and of myself as listener. In contrast, the forms of Buddhist chanting found in China, Tibet, and Japan have a most *unconscious* quality, as does all chanting and ceremonial in so-called "primitive cultures." This is "unconscious" in the Jungian sense, which is to say, arising from the unconscious mind. Early in human history, people had very little awareness of themselves as separate individuals. Identity was based on membership in family, clan, and tribe. Chanting and ritual were the means by which collective wisdom was passed on from generation to generation. The lessons of history, collective experience, and group values were memorized in vast oral traditions. Early Buddhist chants were developed during the latter period of these oral traditions, before writing was commonplace. The chant patterns are rhythmic and repetitive, which aids memorization, and they touch a place very deep in the human psyche. While they also have beauty and power, it is their unconscious simplicity that is most apparent. Engrossed in them, I can sometimes lose the sense of time and place, and of myself as chanter or listener. While the chant patterns have beauty, they were not intended to be compared to other chants and rated as to style, development of themes, etc. This is what makes them so unself-conscious compared to a composition by Mozart. Gregorian chant is a little different from early Buddhist chant. It was developed in Europe during the first few centuries AD and was finally systematized under Pope Gregory I in the 6th Century. It is more melodic and complex than earlier chant forms but retains some of the unconscious quality in that it is a system for applying set chant patterns to lines of verse of various length. So it falls somewhere between the very self-conscious composition of an artist, and the collective efforts that produced the earliest chants.

While listening to the beautiful strains of the *Mass*, I was further struck by the thought that great composers like Mozart strive to reconnect with the unconscious, almost like coming full circle. We have the image, which is practically archetypal, of the muse taking over so that the artist works all night, finally collapses into sleep, exhausted, then wakes to find a masterpiece. This is pretty much how Mozart himself was portrayed in *Amadeus*, when he wrote the *Requiem Mass*. And when it works, the listener too is transported out of self-conscious listening into something deeper. In basketball, when players go on a shooting streak, its called entering a "zone." When they go one step further, continually making fabulous plays and impossible shots, they say they are "unconscious." This is because when they are that hot, they are barely aware of it at all. It's as if a "sports muse" takes over their bodies for a time, performing miraculous feats. Only when they come to do they realize what they've done. Then, of course, it's over.

In our modern world, we are hyper-aware of everything. Media images bombard us constantly so that we have become too conscious—at least of all the *external* details of modern life. What we need is to rediscover the joys of becoming unconscious; that is, less aware of ourselves. With this comes the power to tap into the pulse and throb of life itself, vitalizing our actions. At the same time, we also need to become more conscious of the internal world, bringing into the light of awareness the things that drive us and compel us to act in repetitive and sometimes destructive patterns. Together, this describes our practice of meditation, and I think this is what it means to both wake up, and let go. As Dogen says, "To study the Buddha Way, is to study the self. To study the self, is to forget the self. To forget the self is to be actualized by myriad things."[9] Perhaps we can call our practice the "art of daily life." Awakening to old patterns of behavior that cause suffering and alienation is "studying the self." It is the first step in dissolving the barriers we maintain between ourselves and others. Then, as our practice and mindfulness deepens, we focus more completely on each thing we meet, and each thing we do. We cultivate *single-mindedness*, which means that "mind" and "object," or "self" and "other," are experienced as one. No separation is felt. When we "forget" ourselves this way, the muse we call "Buddha Nature" can take over. It may not seem like a masterpiece, but a well-lived day of practice has tremendous beauty and the power to move others, perhaps even greater than that of a Mozart Mass.

FACING

THE

DRAGON

MIND TO MIND

Remember your adolescent years, and how it felt to be put down for saying something that wasn't cool? How about a little later, lets say college age, when the worst thing that could happen was to be shown up as unsophisticated? Unfortunately, people sometimes try to make themselves feel better by demonstrating some sort of superiority over others. When they can't manage it another way, they may resort to making someone else look inferior. In our culture, the preferred way to do this is with sarcastic or cynical jibes. Sarcasm and cynicism are attitudes of mind that belittle things, people, ideas, or make light of them, in a derogatory way. The inference is that the belittler is in some way above the thing belittled. It is so much 'cooler,' so much more sophisticated, to take this approach than to puff oneself up with crude boasting. But it seems to me that arrogance requires something to be superior to, so the interesting thing is, a simple, straightforward boast contains much less real arrogance than a sarcastic or cynical jibe.

Both 'sarcasm' and 'cynicism' can refer to a variety of things, but I am here using the words to refer to the tendency to turn up one's nose in contempt at anything simple and naive. To me this is the very essence of arrogance. We come into this world uncomplicated and naturally naive, so what changes people so that they wish to express the negative arrogance of sarcasm and cynicism? When we look back at our own first experiences of being put down, even years later, the sarcasm will still sting. When we first experience this incredible behavior, it is always some simple, naive thing that we say or do that sets us up to be put down. It only takes one or two experiences to realize that expressing naiveté around others can be very dangerous. A strong desire to protect ourselves arises, and we start to build a shell of sophistication of our own. But when we do this, we come to distrust our own simple, uncomplicated mind of naiveté. This naive mind is the mind that accepts things at face value, just as they appear. It places no complicated judgement on events but simply experiences them directly, whether pleasant or unpleasant. The naive mind is the childlike mind of wonder, the mind of discovery. To this mind, simple things are always new, and uncomplicated emotions are completely valid. But when we want to project a facade of sophistication, which we cannot integrate with the simple, nonjudgmental mind of naiveté, we come to the point of fearing our naiveté. After all, we have found out the hard way that it can make us vulnerable. So what do we do then? We try to stamp it out, to cut it down whenever it arises within us. But we only succeed in covering it over with sarcasm and cynicism of our own. We can never really outgrow this naive mind, so how can we ever hope to cut it off, for it is part of our own original, natural mind, which is Buddha Mind itself. What we can do is cultivate inner strength through all-acceptance, and this leads to wisdom. In nonjudging acceptance we can experience things directly, and through this, develop a deep understanding of ourselves and our experience. Then the vulnerability of naiveté is transcended and transformed into empathy.

Most of the time, however, we cover up the naive mind with a layer of sarcasm to hide our fear and embarrassment. Protected in this way, or so we think, with a shield of sophisication, we venture into the world unafraid. But an interesting thing happens. Whenever someone around us expresses naiveté, the simple naive mind inside of us responds to it in an echo of empathy. This causes our fear of vulnerability to surface again, and we feel compelled to cut down this dangerous and irrepressible naiveté whenever, and wherever, it arises. We do this as an instinct to protect ourselves, and we end up putting down others exactly the way others put us down before. This need to put down others with sarcastic or cynical comments arises, really, because of that fear. The *desire* to feel superior arises later, as an afterthought. At first we put down others simply because we fear participating in something "uncool," but the step from there to putting down others in order to feel superior ourselves follows very quickly. But really, the arrogance of cynicism is a by-product of fear. The fact that we feel the need to cut down naiveté arising in others is very important, though. When we are with someone who expresses naiveté, it *is* felt within ourselves, and our own uncomplicated and naive mind arises in response. This is a demonstration of the One

Mind of enlightenment. It is a Buddhist teaching that we are always, at every moment, feeling and expressing this One Mind. But a mind unawakened to its own innate enlightenment merely reacts to things automatically and out of habit, in ways that usually create suffering. Naiveté arising in someone else will be treated in the same way that we treat it arising in ourselves. If we fear it, we will cut it down, perhaps with a sarcastic jibe. In its own negative way, this expresses enlightenment. Causing pain in another person, just as we felt it in ourselves before, the need to protect ourselves with a facade of sophistication is passed on anew. This negative transmission from mind to mind exists because we are, at all times, one with all beings and the limitless universe, and because the everyday mind is originally and innately one with enlightenment.

To be *aware* of enlightenment, to discover and know it, is to discover again the naive mind of a child. It is to take delight again in things simple and honest. The mind of enlightenment is nonjudgmental, yet responsible and discerning. It empathizes easily with others, even those quite different from ourselves, and with those who are being foolish or silly. Can we accept empathy at such times? In the mind of enlightenment there is empathy even with people being selfish and cruel; not with their compulsion to cruelty, but with the suffering that they themselves feel beneath that compulsion. It can also empathize with those expressing sarcasm and cynicism; not in sharing the facade, but in knowing why it was built. It can be frightening to face the mind of enlightenment, because it means letting down whatever barriers have been built up against becoming vulnerable again. I think it is vitally important to accept this return to vulnerability and to feel the pain that it brings. Despite the pain, part of us is immaculate and untouched. Once we experience that, we know that none of this can *really* hurt us. When we do, we can understand why the greatest strength is expressed in gentleness.

We are always expressing the One Mind of enlightenment whether we know it or not, and our arrogance, cynicism, anger, fear, guilt, and other negative habits of mind are being felt by others in some way every time they pop up. When we consider what that means, we realize we have a responsibility to be careful about what we transmit.

We have a duty, as it were, not to clutter up the airwaves with old junk. Obviously, we can't avoid negative feelings, and I don't want to confuse harmful karmic patterns with something like straightforward, honest anger that arises with great force and purity, like lightning. But Zen practice means to let *all* feelings arise and fall, choosing to stay in touch with the still center of meditation. As we learn to identify more with the still, empty space through which these things pass, we identify with the feelings themselves much less. Then our actions can come from a place of deeper wisdom, instead of from the superficial winds of emotion. Many of our feelings come from karmic conditioning, like the tendency to sarcasm. It is a deeply significant Bodhisattva act to not pass on the unfortunate karma we have inherited from the limitless past. Meditation practice helps us do that. It makes the world just a little bit brighter, and the possibility of joy and freedom just a little bit more evident. It is also true that positive, constructive attitudes of mind can be just as contagious as negative ones. So we can see that at every moment, as we choose either to train or indulge ourselves, we are choosing to transmit something. This is why it is so important to undergo Zen practice with a pure heart and great effort. The Transmission of the Truth from master to disciple is possible because of this very principle. This is a transmission that expresses the deepest enlightenment itself. We are already part of the Great Matter, so we should consider every action with very great care.

THE DRAGON'S JAWS

One, seven, three, five,
Nothing to rely upon in this or any world;
Night falls, and the water is flooded with moonlight;
Here in the Dragon's jaws,
Many exquisite jewels.

Setcho[1]

Magnificent! Magnificent!
No one knows the final word.
The ocean bed's aflame,
Out of the void leap wooden lambs.

Fumon[2]

I can think of no more powerful or beautiful expressions of Zen than these sets of verses. The first, from the early Song period in China, became a sort of mantra for me at one stage of my monastic training. The second is a death poem, composed during Fumon's final hours. It is so very true that no "thing," person, experience, or relationship may be relied upon in any absolute way; and how can we hope to comprehend the very forces that form the human mind? How futile, like a fish trying to swallow the sea. And yet, accepting this truth, sitting within the dragon's jaws, we find such astonishing beauty!

Great Master Dogen once said, "The koan in daily life is will, words are (but) its key."[3] Even in the worldly sense, the secret of a successful life is in making everything work to your advantage. This means making every event an opportunity. A door-to-door salesman is the best example of this I know. A salesman knows that on a good day he will be turned down ten times before he hears "yes." Therefore, when turned down, the best salesmen say to themselves, "Good, I know not to waste any more time here!" and then hurry to the next prospect undaunted. What an excellent example of training. In the religious sense, learning to do this means learning to look up. This is the meaning of "will" in Dogen's teaching. Life will teach us all eventually that we cannot force our wills on events. However, no matter what happens, we can turn our wills towards positivity. Looking up, with brightness of mind, is an option always within our grasp.

Looking up. This is the secret of life. Nothing can ever stop us from being successful when we understand this. But we should, naturally, be prepared to be flexible with our goals; otherwise we can define ourselves into failure. Positivity here does not mean taking a saccharin, "Pollyanna" attitude. Positivity means clarity of mind; it means turning toward the light, toward the truth. The meaning of this teaching is perhaps most clear when facing adversity. In the face of adversity, looking up means sitting up straight, the back erect, eyes open just as we do in zazen. When we do this, we are open to seeing the Dharma within the circumstances right in front of us, whatever they may be.

When my teacher was in Japan, her master, Chisan Koho, inquired if she played chess.

"Yes," she answered.
"Good. How many sound moves can you make?" he asked.
She gave it some thought and answered, "Two," reasoning that one should always think a little ahead.
"Well," he replied, "that's one more than I can manage."

After reflecting, she realized that, of course, no one can make more than one sound move. After all, you can only move one piece at a time and then reassess your plan after your opponent's move. But the significance of this is very great. People often think that they know where they are going when they set out to do something. Some even think that they know where they are going in life. Actually, we never really know. All we can know for certain is how much presence of mind we have as we take each step. That is what Chisan Koho meant by one sound move. Even if we can't know for certain where we are going, in time we can develop a good sense of direction. As we practice Zen, we find that this really sums up daily life. Our efforts always interact with events, other people, and their actions, so that the results are *inevitably* somewhat different from what we had intended. And the truth is, our vision is always a little fuzzy, at best. Think of what it's like to design and create a physical object, even when using the most compliant of materials; or of drawing a picture, or planning a simple social gathering. The end result will always be a little different, for good or ill, than we plan. Is it any wonder then, that in times of adversity, when we must deal with complicated issues and people that have different or conflicting goals, events rarely turn out as we would wish?

> When we work hard to achieve a particular end, it takes great willingness to accept the outcome as it is affected and distorted by events. But willingness and acceptance in the face of adversity are the means we have of growing in wisdom, for it's through this practice that we come to understand the world a little better. It is precisely here, where our own desires and efforts to achieve them conflict with other people and events, that faith, willingness, and wisdom come together through practice. It is especially through adversity that we realize the futility of clinging to our opinions of how things should work out. So when you think you know where you are going, watch out! Far better to have a good sense of direction. After all, there is nothing to rely upon in this or any world. But here in the dragon's jaws, such joy!

❧

I first wrote the words above in the spring of 1986. At that time, living with adversity and learning to practice within it was a matter of intense everyday concern. The period from November 1985 until around June of 1987 was the most difficult Gyokuko and I have ever had to face. Just before this, though, things seemed to be progressing fairly well. We had been living at the center in Eugene, Oregon, when the Sangha in Portland was getting ready to buy a house. We had been running both groups, travelling to Portland every month. We decided to move to Portland from our base in Eugene to help with their relocation. Then, in a six-month period, came the following events: the house purchase was blocked by a rancorous and hysterical neighborhood group; our parent temple announced sweeping organizational changes including completely centralized authority requiring absolute obedience; then they required the Eugene group to sever all connections with the Portland group, and with Gyokuko and me in particular; we were told that we would either have to dissolve our marriage or cease to function as priests, and that one of us would have to return to the monastery; as this was to conform with the standards of a Chinese Buddhist group in Malaysia that previously had no real connection with our parent group, this made little sense to us, and we decided to resign our affiliation but continue as priests; the parent organization appeared to accept this at first, then severed all contact with us, eventually forbidding anyone connected with them to associate with us; a small group split off from our Portland Sangha to maintain affiliation with the parent group, then demanded a share of the temple assets; and to set the stage, our beloved St. Bernard, George, died just as all this started.

It is hard to express the feeling of shock, disbelief, and heartsick pain that overwhelmed us and many of our Sangha members in those days. With so much going wrong at one time, Gyokuko and I had to look deeply at ourselves. Were we reaping the consequences of our own karma? We certainly made our share of mistakes in the midst of all the turmoil. When we looked deeply within ourselves, however, we knew two things. First, being priests is not just something we do, it is who we are. Second, we are deeply committed to our marriage, and it is very important to our practice. So it was perfectly clear to us what we had to do. At one point, though, we thought we would simply leave Portland and start a little independent temple somewhere else. But the majority of the members had stood behind us, and they made it clear that we would be abandoning them if we left. Yet who wants to come to a temple racked with dissention and political turmoil? Membership and participation dropped off. In a situation like that, there are no choices that are free of negative consequences. In the end, we decided to stick it out, as cold and bitter as it was. I remember one morning in particular, when we realized that staying or leaving would be essentially the same, and we would just have to sit in our little zendo, whether anyone else chose to come or not. I can't possibly describe how comforting it was to rest in the certainty of that one decision.

It was in the middle of all this turmoil and anxiety that I thought of Setcho's words: "One, seven, three, five, nothing to rely upon in this or any world." For months we had tried to make things work out, to keep our connection with our parent temple, yet stay true to our vows as we made them. But everything we tried seemed to throw fuel on the flames. "Night falls, and the water is flooded with moonlight." In such dark times, that one simple decision to sit in our zendo brought a flood of tranquility. But it didn't change our circumstances much at all. "Here in the dragon's jaws, many exquisite jewels." Looking back on it now, it seems as if much of the disaster was inevitable. Conditions inherent in our parent organization were leading toward centralization and the retraction of authority previously granted, just as our local group was starting to come into its own. Our former parent organization is now more authoritarian than the Vatican, with total power resting in one person. No one else may ever teach of their own authority, which is completely contradictory to what we were taught there. As all this played out, it seemed as if everything we had worked for, everything we had hoped to accomplish, was crushed by an avalanche of opposition. It can be very difficult to see anything positive in some events. I think that trying to do so can be an obstacle in itself, for when we fail, there is little option but despair. When we succumb to despair and mourn what might have been, we miss the exquisite beauty that is always all around us. Some events are, to us, tragic. But they are just events. The pain we feel is real. But it is just sensation. For me, grasping the will and looking up meant sitting alone in the zendo. Then, such unspeakable beauty.

In December of 1987, almost exactly a year after our Conditional Use permission was reversed on appeal, we closed the sale on our present house. At about that time, we heard the news that the Neighborhood Association that had worked to block our previous purchase had lost its city charter. There had been a bitter dispute within the group, and they had refused to accept the city's arbitration. We found out that our previous proposal had reignited a long running battle in that area over an unimproved lot, and that we were, in essence, walking into an old family fight. What is more, if we had beaten the appeal and moved into the neighborhood, we would have been tied to a mortgage that was countersigned by members who ended up splitting off to stay with the parent organization. Today we are in a much better location, with better facilities than we would have had there. When we were cut off from our parent monastery and our own teacher, I felt like we had been pushed off a cliff. Sitting still in our little zendo, I knew our only choice was to fly. Independence has been difficult, but also incredibly rewarding. Our temple has had to grow up, become a center for practice in its own right, and learn how to meet the needs of the members in ways it never did before. Now we must find the Dharma within ourselves, without looking elsewhere. Today our membership is about three times what is was when the split occurred, and we have added a church building to our facilities. The membership has grown in intangible ways too, as individuals mature and accept new challenges. As it has turned out, we are accomplishing everything we had hoped for, and more, but by a route we could not even have imagined. At this point I can say with some certainty that I have no idea where we are going from here. But I hope that together we continue to make one sound move at a time, and develop a good sense of direction.

For me, the real lesson in all this is not about "right" and "wrong," or "success" and "failure." It is about remembering what really matters. It is about being true to ourselves, and always moving toward the Dharma, for at the very heart of it—that is what we really want. While it is vitally important to try to do what is right and ethical, some decisions just cannot be reached on that level. "Magnificent! magnificent! No one knows the final word." In the midst of turmoil and adversity, reason and the conscious mind can be left floundering. Where are we to turn? The real answer is not an "answer," and it lies deep in the place where the question arises. "The ocean bed's aflame. Out of the void leap wooden lambs."

ABSOLUTELY VITAL LIFE

"The life of this one day, today, is absolutely vital life. . ."[4] With these words, found in *Shushogi*, Dogen is telling us to look closely and carefully at our own lives, just as they are, to understand the meaning of Buddhist practice. He is addressing our tendency to long for some ideal circumstance, far away in time or space, and which is very different from our own daily lives, where our innate potential for enlightenment will burst forth easily. For some, this longing leads to endless searching for the right teacher, the right practice, the right community. For others, it means trying to make the world conform to their ideals by insisting their spouse, workplace, or religious community shape up and provide the necessary qualities. But this obstacle can take another form after we have embraced practice wholeheartedly. We compound our difficulty when we think we have found something special, a way of living "everyday life" that is different and better than other kinds of "everyday life." In a way it's true, too, which is why the problem is so tricky. When we start meditation, clean up our act, get more in harmony with the Precepts and so forth, we know we have made real improvements. But then we can start to see some things as outside this practice and so "impure." While we need to guard ourselves against the pull of old habit-energy, we should be careful of this dualistic thinking.

I had spent ten years in Zen monastic practice, and Gyokuko seven, when we got married in 1982 and moved up here to Portland, taking on this little temple. The monastery we had come from was steeped in the renunciate tradition, and life there was very monastic and otherworldly. Moving from a rural monastery in the mountains of Northern California to an urban temple that focused on lay practice was quite a challenge. At first we felt as if we had landed on another planet. In the midst of city life, with its pace, noise, and aggression, it seemed that our practice was foreign; that it took place only within our little temple, and "outside" was hostile territory where we just survived. One day when Gyokuko and I were still pretty new to

Portland, I took our dog, George, for a walk. The temple in those days was in what is called a transitional neighborhood. It was between a fairly upscale, almost all white area, and one of the worst slums, almost all black. Our neighborhood was racially mixed, which was very nice at times, but it was also a point of racial tension. Getting to know the rules was another adjustment for us. On this particular walk, George lifted his leg *near* a rose bush planted in the strip between the street and the side-walk. All of a sudden, from over the fence, I was hit by a spray of water. "Hey!" I yelled, just as another spray came, then another. As I scrambled out of range with George, I caught a glimpse through a hedge of an elderly black woman trying to stay out of sight while wielding the hose. We went on our way, but as we walked, I began quietly to steam. As someone who carefully picked up after his dog, I had tired of taking abuse because of those that did not. In previous weeks Gyokuko and I had encountered real hostility just for *having* a dog, which was very hard to understand, and these confrontations had a lot to do with why the world outside our little temple felt alien and antagonistic. Those who don't have dogs often don't understand that dogs need to be walked, and that's when they tend to "go." Because there were loose and sometimes vicious dogs in the neighborhood, I had to pick my route for walking George very carefully. It was beginning to feel as though there was no option open to me that wouldn't draw flak. All this went through my mind as I walked. Now, a monastery is a very close community, so problems that arise between people have to be worked out. But because cities have grown so anonymous, aggression has become misplaced, and oddly impersonal. All of a sudden, while on that walk, I realized that I lived in that neighborhood. Perhaps that sounds silly. But it was then that I knew I had to go talk to that woman. At first she was reluctant. But eventually she explained her point of view, and I explained mine. On one level we resolved nothing. But we met eye to eye and came to an understanding. I remember looking out over the neighborhood from the front porch of the Zen Center when I returned. At that moment I realized that this was now my monastery, and that everyday life in that often difficult neighborhood was my teacher.

One of the finest chapters of Dogen's *Shobogenzo* is a very short one called "Shoji,"[5] which means "Birth and Death." In it, he stresses that each moment is both a becoming and a passing away, so each moment contains both birth and death. When I think about this deeply, it strikes me as profoundly true. In each breath there is both arising and falling, coming and going, and this is birth and death. So each moment is absolutely *vital* life, and in every instant there is absolutely vital Truth. Each moment, then, is deeply significant. As this is so, what part of our own lives cannot be considered absolutely vital to practice? Sometimes we may think, "My work is my practice," or "My art is my practice," or "Raising my children, now that's where my practice really lies." Sometimes we can only see formally sitting in zazen as practice. While all of these things are excellent to do, and each is an important arena for practice, if we wish to understand the "absolutely vital life" of this one day, then we should take up the challenge to see every moment and every experience as an expression of deep truth.

Part of the rhythm of life in a Zen monastery is Shosan, the ceremonial question and answer done on the 1st and 15th days of each month. In this ceremony, one of the Senior monks with teaching responsibilities stands before the altar after morning service, incense is burned, then all the Junior monks in training come forward one at a time, bow, and ask a question. The Junior monks have been preparing their questions for several days. Each one is supposed to express the essence of their practice and understanding, or the essence of their doubts, in the form of a very brief, highly condensed question. The Senior monk should be prepared to hear the *essence* of each question, then give an answer from the depths of her own meditation. The idea is that in time the Juniors learn to hear the answer arising within themselves even as they ask the question. So when the Senior prepares to stand before the altar and answer questions at Shosan, she must look deeply within to get past all opinions, all judgments of self and others, to be ready for the questions that arise. Because no matter what a question sounds like, it contains the question What is Truth? The preparation done by the Senior monk at the altar is really the same as that done by the Junior monks before they ask their questions.

The one who asks and the one who answers must each look beneath appearances, focus their minds, and be prepared to leap beyond the trap of habitual thinking. It takes great effort to loose the bonds of self and truly meet another person face to face.

It was a major turning point for me when I decided to face that angry woman who sprayed me with the hose. What *was* her gesture, if not a deeply-felt need to communicate? To know that we *are* one with everything around us, and to know, in a deep and vital way, our utter oneness with every being that comes before us means that we must learn to see this unity even when the one in front of us is pushing all our buttons, or is whining and manipulative, or is unpleasant, cranky, and confrontational. Touching this unity is not always a blissful experience, but we *can* learn to truly face an arrogant employer, a frustrated and angry clerk, or a drunken panhandler. When we do, we recognize the moment in front of us *is* absolutely vital Truth. For me this means being willing to see the hassle of everyday life as Shosan. When I do this, each pain-in-the-neck of daily life becomes a Bodhisattva on the path of Truth, and every moment *is* absolutely vital life. After all, it is literally true that no matter what someone says, no matter how badly he or she behaves, the person is really asking, "What is the meaning of our meeting? Is there oneness now? What is the Dharma of this moment?" An obscene gesture from a passing motorist, a racial taunt, a mugging, and even, so help me, rape and murder are asking, each in their own distorted way, about the truth of Zen.

In Tang China, the monk Hyakujo was walking with his master, Baso, when a wild duck rose up suddenly in front of them and flew off. When Baso asked, "What was that?" Hyakujo answered, "A wild duck." Then Baso asked, "Where did it go?" and Hyakujo answered, "It flew away." Baso then grabbed him by the nose, gave it a tweak, and said, "Has it, really? Why, it's been here all along."[6] My teacher compared this story with a popular tale about Martin Luther. As the story goes, the devil appeared to Luther in the midst of the flames in his fireplace one night. Luther took the fireplace tongs and grabbed the devil by the nose, saying, "If you can speak a word of truth, I'll let you go!" The devil yelled "Ow!" Luther replied, "Good enough," released him, and the devil vanished.[7] The koan of everyday life is that we are one with, and part of, everything that comes before us. That's why Baso tweaked Hyakujo's nose; where else could the bird be, but right here? Because of this, we participate in all the events that occur around us, whether wonderful or horrible, no matter what we do. When trying things happen, it's as if a Zen Master, much like Luther, grabs us by the nose demanding, "Quick, say a word of Zen." Wherever we live is our monastery, and daily life, just as it is, is that Zen Master, and a very good one. Can you answer? Are you willing to see the very deep significance presented to you within each moment? In each situation can you say a word of Zen? An aggressive gesture tempts us to make an aggressive *counter* gesture. We could just ignore it instead, but doesn't that express superiority, looking down our noses at the other person? Either way we cut the Truth in two. The question has been asked. Can we respond without duality and know absolutely vital life? Or will we join the dance of separate selves and lose the life of Zen?

If we can recognize an aggressive gesture or sharp words as Shosan—the question "What is Truth?"—then we can cut through duality and any answer we give, any response we make, will be a true one. Why? Because within the answer there will be recognition of the Buddha-hood of the one who asks. Sometimes a good verbal clout on the nose is necessary to help someone see their rudeness. Done with centeredness and full awareness of the other person, the Truth is not cut. But we might also walk away without a word, and that too can be a true answer. If we walk away from our anger and judgmentalism rather than our deep connection with the other person, we leave our bond with that person intact. In such an action there is a deep embracing of Buddha Nature.

Some time ago a student of mine was upset. When I asked her about it, she told me that as she was walking home from work she saw a man playing with a puppy near the river beneath the bridge she was crossing. She stopped to watch them for a moment. This student is an animal lover and a rescuer of lost dogs. When the man saw her watching them, he called out to her, asking if she would like to take the puppy, since otherwise he would just abandon it there. As she was in no position to take in another dog at that time, she declined and left feeling angry and depressed that people could be so cruel. When she had related the story to me, she asked why an innocent puppy should suffer because of a stupid person. I don't remember exactly what I said to her in reply, but apparently it included a comment about the fact that puppies and babies sometimes die. Later she came to me, angered at my comment, which she felt was very cold-hearted. The fact was that I did not take her feelings lightly, and we had another long talk. My perception was that her strong feelings for animals were only a part of the depression she was experiencing. We cannot prevent all the suffering of animals, children, or any sentient being, no matter how hard we try. Therefore, it seemed to me that her real issue had less to do with addressing the helpless condition of animals than with addressing the man under the bridge. For some time, whenever we talked about this incident, and the koan it represents, she would call the story "The Puppy Under the Bridge," while to me it was always "The Man Under the Bridge." Over time, she began to understand more of my point. As I see it, the Zen Master of Daily Life had her by the nose. The question is not unlike that of Nansen's when he held up the cat.[*] If you were she, how would you answer?

Here are two Zen stories about confrontations in daily life:

Muso (1275-1351) was a Japanese Rinzai monk, and the National Teacher, so one of the most illustrious masters of his era. One day he left the capital in the company of a disciple for a distant province. On reaching the Tenryu River, they had to wait for an hour before boarding the ferry. Just as it was about to leave the shore, a drunken samurai ran up and leapt into the packed boat, nearly swamping it. He tottered wildly as the small craft made its way across the river, and fearing for the safety of the passengers, the ferryman begged him to stand quietly.

---

[*]In this story, Nansen, who is Abbot, hears monks from different quarters of the monastery arguing about possession of a cat. Nansen goes outside, takes the cat, holds up a knife and says, "Oh monks! If one of you can say a word of Zen I will spare the cat. If you can't say anything, I will put it to the sword." For a translation and commentary on this story, see *Gateless Gate*, Koan Yamada, Center Publications, Los Angeles, 1979, pp. 76–79.

"We're like sardines in here!" the samurai said gruffly. Then, pointing to Muso, "Why not toss out the bonze?" (an impolite term for a monk).

"Please be patient," Muso said. "We'll reach the other side soon."

"What!" bawled the samurai. "Me be patient? Listen here, if you don't jump off this thing and start swimming, I swear I'll drown you!"

The master's continued calm so infuriated the samurai that he struck Muso's head with his iron fan, drawing blood. Muso's disciple had had enough by this time, and as he was a powerful man, wanted to challenge the samurai on the spot. "I can't permit him to go on living after this," he said to the master.

"Why get so worked up over a trifle?" Muso said with a smile. "It's exactly in matters of this kind that the monk's training proves itself. Patience, you must remember, is more than just a word." He then recited an extempore poem:

> *The beater and the beaten:*
> *Mere players of a game*
> *Ephemeral as a dream.*

When the boat reached shore and Muso and his disciple got off, the samurai ran up and prostrated himself at the master's feet. Then and there he became Muso's disciple.[8]

One evening as Shichiri Kojun was reciting sutras, a thief with a sharp sword entered, demanding either his money or his life. Shichiri told him: "Do not disturb me. You can find the money in that drawer." Then he resumed his recitation. A little while afterwards he stopped and called: "Don't take it all. I need some to pay taxes with tomorrow." The intruder gathered up most of the money and started to leave."Thank a person when you receive a gift," Shichiri added. The man thanked him and made off.

A few days afterwards, the fellow was caught and confessed, among others, the offense against Shichiri. When Shichiri was called as a witness, he said: "This man is no thief, at least as far as I am concerned. I gave him the money and he thanked me for it."

After he finished his prison term, the man went to Shichiri and became his disciple.[9]

In the first story, the samurai was so moved by the famous monk's patience that when he realized what he had done, he repented deeply and changed. What really strikes me about this story, though, is that when they were in the boat, nothing the monk did or said had any real effect on the drunken samurai. When we do our best to avoid falling into the pit of opposition, we should not expect miracles. For the most part, people will not be transformed by their encounters with us. My guess is that for every story like this one, there are a hundred in which the drunken samurai stomps off, perhaps wondering a bit, but basically unchanged for the time being. In the second story, the monk refuses to be cowed by the thief. His strength and presence of mind affected the thief enough that he recognized someone who could teach him. But in both cases, the monks did not take the bait and fall into the trap of opposition. Neither did they lose their centeredness and certainty. This is just how koans work. So the challenge in the koan of daily life lies not so much in answering another's question, but in answering our own. The question asked by the Zen Master of daily life, as it takes hold of us by the nose, is "Can you see the truth now? Can you say a word of Zen?" The miracle of Zen practice is that, in reaching down deep for a response that is true to ourselves *and* beyond duality, we find ways of responding that were hidden to us before. Within these responses we may find the best answers of all, ones that hit the mark for both self and other. Offered without expectation, our actions can help heal the rift of duality both for ourselves and for others as well. To make such an answer, we must first drop the self in all-acceptance to meet the other face-to-face. But then we must *act* from this place beyond self if we want the *life* of Zen. Strangely enough, in this action we become ourselves fully. Becoming ourselves fully, we engage life fully, whether we bring to it the roar of a lion or Kanzeon's gentle touch. When every moment is absolutely vital life, our own lives are the Life of the Buddha, moving through us, as us, in a wonderful dance of Truth.

A Dog, a Cat, & a Deathbed:
Distractions & the Deeper Mind

One day a few years ago I was working by myself at the Temple on a very quiet day, but part way through the morning, a dog started barking. This was not half-hearted woofing. This was constant, frantic, loud, and intense barking. As time went on, I was amazed that he could keep it up with such intensity. After about forty minutes he became hoarser and hoarser, and I started to lose my ability to concentrate on what I was doing. I felt a mix of irritation and genuine concern for the noisy mutt. So, I decided to put aside my work and look into the problem. I discovered that the dog was cooped up in a tiny pen in the back yard of the Dharma House, just up the street, where several Sangha members were living together. In the back of my mind, I had felt some annoyance at the person responsible for the dog, but this made no sense. No one living there even owned a dog. Just then, Jim approached from the front of the house, looking somewhat sheepish. He explained that the dog belonged to a neighbor who was at work, that he had got loose, and now he, Jim, was trying to take care of the dog until the neighbor came home. So there he was, saddled with this frantic dog that he had no other way to deal with, while the whole neighborhood was being driven slowly insane. Strangely enough, though, I found it comforting just to understand the situation. At least I knew that the dog was all right, and that everyone was doing the best they could. The distraction I had felt at the dog's barking was greatly reduced.

I left Jim with the noisy mutt to go sit on the front porch at the Temple for a while and enjoy the sun. The neighbor's big orange tomcat came over, as he often did, to say hello and sit on my lap. We sat there together for a bit in great contentment. Meanwhile, the dog barked on. I thought to myself how deeply that cat sat in samadhi, for the frantic yapping of the dog flowed over him with no effect. Then, quite suddenly, there was a little noise made by another cat creeping through the ivy nearby. The cat on my lap started, then lifted his head, and his body tensed. From then on, he kept one ear cocked toward the sounds made by that other cat, and he did not relax again. All at once I understood the reason this cat was able to sit peacefully, completely unaffected by the barking of the dog. In his single enlightenment,[10] the barking had little or no meaning for him. But the sound of that other cat was a very different story.

It is our curse, but also our blessing, as human beings, to be self-conscious; literally, aware of ourselves. It is this ability that leads to the delusion of duality between self and other. But it is also because of this ability that we can become aware of others as fundamentally the same as we are, even as we experience their great differences. Dogen says that to be able to identify oneself with that which is *not* oneself is the true meaning of sympathy, or *identity action,* and this is one of four kinds of wisdom that benefit others, a function of enlightenment itself.[11] In other words, it is enlightenment *with* others. The dog's frantic barking had meaning for me, and for every human being on the block, and that was why it was so distracting. After all, it was a distress call. When we do our zazen practice, we tend to be distracted the most by the sound of a nearby television, children playing, even barking dogs. Oddly enough, this is because the natural functioning of enlightenment connects us deeply and personally to these sounds, and therefore we find *meaning* in them. The mental idiocy we indulge in when such things arise, however, is because of our karma, bad habits, and lack of concentration. To touch samadhi in the midst of all conditions, it is necessary to fully accept conditions as they are. One of the things to accept is that certain things *are* more distracting than others, and with good reason. The sound of a stream, even traffic or mechanical noises, can be conducive to meditation. But a conversation in the next room, or the everyday sounds of our own children, call to us because they have such deep meaning. To meditate deeply under circumstances like these, let the meaning and the pull it has on you arise and pass as something in itself. It will do you little good to try to shut it out or ignore it. That would be like trying to stop your thoughts. In time the pull of distraction dies down, just as thoughts eventually become quiet. Then, if something important should arise that really does demand your immediate attention, you will know that it is time to get up from zazen. Do we really need to get up or not? Does the kids' squabble really require our intervention? As we begin to find the answers to these questions, we start to understand the difference between attachment to things going on around us and just being aware and responsible.

At a retreat some time ago, one of the retreatants complained about the amount of noise from the street and asked for advice on meditating in a noisy city environment. Another one piped up to say that to him, the sound of traffic was pure peace and quiet. It turned out that this second man was an ornithologist living deep in the woods, where he was part of an Oregon State University field study on wildlife. He was doing one of the early studies on the Spotted Owl. He lived out there alone and would get up early every morning to do zazen. Now, early morning is a very active time for birds, and as he was there to study their behavior, each sound they made had meaning for him. He knew exactly what every chirp and flutter of activity meant. What most of us would experience as the "peaceful sounds of nature" was for him a whole soap opera of drama and activity unfolding. He said that coming into the city was "getting away from it all" where he could find some peace and quiet to do some deep meditation.

Of course it is excellent to get away from distractions in order to deepen our meditation, but it is also excellent practice to learn to meditate within distracting circumstances. In fact, sitting in a quiet meditation hall just off a noisy street is a perfect analogy to finding our own still centers in everyday city life. So it can be excellent practice to do zazen with a bit of noise around. My own teacher used to extol the virtues of a little temple near Berkeley that lay in the shadow of a freeway interchange ramp. Sitting in the meditation hall virtually underneath the constant flow of traffic was a perfect parallel to finding the still place of meditation within ourselves that lies beneath the thoughts, emotions, desires, etc., that come and go like so much traffic on a bridge. So, perhaps it does little good to label some circumstances as "good" for meditation, and others as "bad." After all, almost anything can become distracting given the right conditions.

A number of years ago I had the opportunity to do a meditation period I will never forget. I sat with a group of people visiting a woman in the hospital. It was a warm summer night, and the door was wide open. My seat was in full view of the door, and I was aware that I would look fairly strange in my zazen position, sitting stock still in the semi-darkness. There was a little supply cart situated to one side of the door, just out of view. A group of nurses took a long break by the cart and chattered aimlessly and endlessly about trivia. One complained with annoyance about a set of keys someone kept misplacing. All in all, not the most ideal circumstance for meditation. But the woman in the hospital bed was in the final stages of terminal cancer. Through the course of her illness, all the things we take for granted in life were taken from her; her work, family relationships, strength, even her ability to take in food and to choose the time and place for the simplest events in her life. All this she had accepted, and she was ready to die. In letting go of everything taken from her, she had focused her mind on one thing. Her entire existence seemed poised on the edge of the absolute, with all externals stripped away. Sitting there with her that evening was a remarkable experience. The nurses outside pouring trivia in through the door seemed to exist in complete independence from the monumental event taking place in front of me in that neither one really affected the other. Perhaps it would be better to say that neither one stood against the other; there was absolutely no conflict between them. Someone that near death is focused totally on the moment, and on the absolute within the moment, for that is absolutely all there is. Everything else ceases to have meaning. For the nurses, daily life had to go on. Working in a hospital means putting one foot in front of the other, meeting each demand, just living, and being human. Dogen says that when life comes there is only life; when death comes there is only death.[12] In the hallway, there was only life; in the bed, there was only death.

From my vantage point in the corner of the room, I seemed to be poised halfway between the two. On one side there was the awesome stillness of death, the absolute. On the other was the clatter and chatter of daily life, the relative. It was one of those moments that vividly reveals the natural harmony of everything. As we do our sitting practice, working to be centered and focused within ourselves, idle chatter in the next room can be very distracting. But as I sat in that hospital room, "distraction" had no meaning. We should use peace and quiet to good advantage to cultivate concentration. But when we think that meditation depends upon external conditions in some fundamental way, we cut enlightenment in two and risk losing our practice whenever conditions are not ideal, right when we need it the most. But holding the mind bright, finding clarity within each moment as it arises, we begin to really understand the perfection that lies within it. Every moment becomes an opportunity for enlightenment.

> *One minute of sitting, one inch of Buddha.*
> *Like lightning all thoughts come and pass.*
> *Just once look into your own mind depths:*
> *Nothing else has ever been.*
> *Manzan Dohaku*[13]

REMEMBRANCE

Some time ago, a Zen Center member came to tell us that a woman he was very close to had been killed in an accident. There was to be a Remembrance Gathering at the school where she had been a faculty member. Although she had been very close to the Zen Center member, most of us had met her only once, quite briefly. Listening to students, faculty, and old friends remark upon the effects she had had on their lives, I perceived something in a rather new light. I never really knew her, yet I could see and feel the effect her life had on these people. I think it can be said that the truest measure of the human heart is the impression it leaves on those it has touched.

In the early years at the monastery, when we were building the first stretch of cloister between the Abbot's quarters and the main house, we found that there were two cherry trees directly in the path of the structure. At the time, the trees were very ill, and it was doubtful whether they would last much longer. But in debating what to do, it was decided to build the cloister around the trees and connect to the main house in a way other than originally planned. In so doing, we created a little nook formed by the cloister wall. As it turned out, the trees recovered and came back as strong as ever. It struck me at the time, however, that when those trees do die, the nook in the cloister will remain as a tribute to their having been there, and to the way we felt about them. I think it is the same way with people. When someone who is close to us leaves this world, it is like removing a press mold from wet clay. The impression left upon us by all the ways they touched us is the truest measure of their having lived. In *Life After Life*,[14] by Raymond Moody, it is revealed that people who have near death experiences report that they are asked a question as they approach death that amounts to "What have you done with your life?" They also report that this question has nothing to do with what they have built or accumulated, but with how they have touched other living things. When facing the great matter of life and death, all questions dissolve into one fundamental question, and this is the essential point of religion. Yet it is in the manner that we live our everyday lives, in all the myriad little details and choices we make, that we put the religious life to the test. It is here that we touch and affect other people. It was so very clear to me at the Remembrance Gathering that this had been a person whose heart was full and good, and that she lived on in the hearts of those she touched.

When faced with death, we suddenly gain perspective on what matters. We reflect upon how fragile life is, and, for a moment, we remember, love, and respect all those who have touched our lives. It is an excellent meditation to consider how we ourselves would like to be remembered when our own time comes.

THE MONSTER
OF MYTHIC PROPORTIONS

The image of a hero facing a crucial test is a classic one in mythology. He may have to face a monster like a sphinx, or endure some great hardship. In the great matter the hero is undertaking, those who fail the test are turned to stone or burned to ashes. The point of these trials is that it takes both great courage of heart *and* nobility of purpose to pass the test of a true hero. It occurred to me recently that tests like this come to us everyday. But rather than as monsters of mythic proportion, they appear in the form of other normal people. In Zen practice our seniors and teachers often have exactly this role to play for us. But since they are simply people, it is easy to blame them when *we* fail the test. When a senior corrects someone for being noisy or distracting to others during a retreat, the hero bows and accepts the correction—regardless of mitigating circumstances—and jumps beyond praise and blame. That seems easy enough to do when we visualize such a scenario from a comfortable distance. We can imagine ourselves bowing nobly, with no concern for praise or blame. After all, from this perspective we can see it really doesn't matter. But when such things happen to us in real life, we find ourselves facing another limited human being. All our opinions about who this person is and our perceptions of his or her shortcomings rise up before us. *This*, perhaps, is the monster of mythic proportions, for here we have the crucial moment of the test. Falling into the pit of duality, we will be burned to ashes; or, bowing in acceptance, we can leap beyond praise and blame, self and other.

Great Master Dogen speaks of finding the Buddha within birth and death.[15] What *is* birth and death other than the arising and disappearing of the self? And what is being trapped in praise and blame, other than being caught in attachment to self? With praise the self arises as our illusions are affirmed. Then comes blame, and the self collapses as our illusions are shattered. Simply accepting the mortality of the limited self, we can touch something greater. This is finding the Buddha within birth and death. There is a Zen saying that when the master asks a question, the disciple that cannot answer should be beaten; and the disciple that *can* answer should be beaten. A related saying is that a disciple must be worthy to be beaten. This can sound pretty sadistic and, in fact, has been the basis of abuse, but the beating referred to here is a testing as to whether or not the disciple can jump beyond praise and blame. To be considered ready for such a test is to be deemed very worthy. I want to make it very clear that there is a time for such testing, a time when the disciple's limits are pushed quite hard. Needless to say, treating disciples like this should never become a way of life for the master or any senior. Even so, in the relationship of master to disciple, the disciple will find himself tested in this way throughout his life. The way he responds shows the level of his understanding.

This brings me to the question of surrender, which is a matter of great importance. My own teacher told me that the disciple should never give her will over to her master. It was very important for me to hear this teaching. But what I also had to understand in time was that surrender of the ego *is* the entry way to the path of training. I once read that the famous Genpo Roshi said that the Gateless Gate is nothing other than the barrier of our own pride. This is the "gate that is not a gate." When we take a teacher, we are asking to pass through this barrier, so sometimes the role of the teacher is to be the obstacle our pride must encounter. When we surrender the ego in this encounter, it is not a surrender to the teacher, but to the Buddha; to Truth itself; to God. Still, it is *through* the teacher that we do this. "Surrendering to God" in our own minds, as it were, is almost easy, but surrendering to the Buddha in the form of "life as it is" is very hard. We can only do this in real life situations, such as facing the teacher. The teacher, after all, is just a human being. But surrendering in the presence of something tangible, a real live human being that can witness the surrender, is what makes the surrender real.

In my own experience, I found that I had to surrender in this way over and over again. I had to learn surrender as a mode of being. Ultimately, this practice led to the greatest release when I surrendered—that is really bowed—to my teacher's shortcomings. Yet still I did not give my will over to my teacher. In surrender I gave it up to the Buddha. Surrendering over and over, we gradually develop a relationship to the teacher largely freed of ego involvement. As this freedom develops, the time of Dharma Transmission is near. But still the disciple is tested further. Dharma Battle is when master and disciple express themselves fully, and the dross of ego burns away, as in a refiners fire. When both stand clear-eyed together, then certification can take place. The Chinese Zen Master Rinzai talked of "Four Distinctions"[16] in the way he taught disciples. Drawing a parallel to this, first a teacher uses praise to encourage a new disciple. Next she adds blame, using a "carrot" and "stick" approach to sharpen the disciples awareness of self. Then she focuses on blame to propel the student past attachment to self, and the duality of praise and blame. Finally, she uses neither praise nor blame whenever master and disciple stand together naturally, just as themselves.

One of my Lay Disciples told a story once about being at a public talk by a prominent and very senior monk in a non-Buddhist tradition, who is well known for his strict discipline. As the talk was about to begin, a nun in training with him did something to displease him. He took her to task, severely chastising her for five minutes or longer as the whole assembly looked on. The Lay Disciple in attendance was quite upset, as he could see tears in the nun's eyes. Then he noticed that she was transfixed in a sort of ecstacy. When I first heard that story, I thought, "Now that's scary. There's a line you should not cross." Some time later Gyokuko and I were out camping. One morning we were getting ready to leave for a day of hiking, and, during the process, I did something to step on her toes. She have me a good verbal whack, and I bristled. But I sat still with it. It can be a useful practice to just sit still and refrain from reacting when things happen that we don't like. I find I'm often able to deal with things much better when I do that. For a while, as we headed out on our hike, that's how I handled the situation with Gyokuko. But with a little time, I came to the point of recognizing my own resistance, and I just let it go. I released my attachment to opinion, and as I did, I surrendered. I felt the rigidity of self melt away, and my heart begin to warm. Then I remembered that nun and realized that yes, there can be great value in chastisement. While it can be painful, it is the quick way past praise and blame, self and other. Now that Gyokuko and I have assumed roles as teachers for various people in our little center, it is important that it be known that we are subject to this practice, too. We are not above correction. Besides accepting this from each other, both of us often feel chastised by this group, even though the master-disciple relationship is not an equal one. I think many people don't realize the degree to which teachers feel themselves to be disciplined through their work with the Sangha, and the degree to which they take it to heart.

As Buddhism is transplanted to the west, mistakes and problems can occur in the attempt to bring traditions like the one I am describing into a new cultural setting. Centers all over America have had problems due to misunderstandings or to the unchecked abuse of power that can arise when a teacher is isolated and has no peer group. When I look back on the way Gyokuko and I presented Zen practice when we first came to Oregon, I see how much we emphasized that there is no surrender to another person, and that surrender is largely to circumstances, to "life as it is." After all, this is how practice actually works for most lay people, and we wanted to avoid making the same mistakes we had seen. I have noticed a similar emphasis in the way other second generation Zen teachers present practice. I think many of us have seen the same sort of mistakes made. But now I can see that in trying to circumvent some of the problems that cropped up in my own circumstances, I have avoided discussing what surrender means when face-to-face with another human being. No, we do not surrender to another person. But it is almost impossible to understand what real surrender is until it is done in relationship to another human being. This is a very difficult distinction to make.

I once heard a story about a Western woman's experience in Japan. She was in a unique situation that was both wonderful and very difficult. She trained as a monk in a very large monastery that is one of the head temples of the Soto Sect. She was the only foreigner, and the only woman in an old and venerable institution. There were those in the temple who were very much opposed to her being there, and they could be quite pointed in making their feelings known. The monastery was designed for men only, there were no women's bathrooms or lavatories, for example, so she was constantly put in awkward situations. Baths in Japan are a rather formal matter, with cleansing done in one part of the bathhouse, then bathing itself done in large, very hot soaking tubs. The bathhouse accommodates a number of people at one time. In the monastery, everything is done in strict order of rank. A rota was posted indicating the times on bath days when monks of various positions could use the bathhouse. Naturally, there was no provision for women. This presented a bit of a problem. The woman noticed that there was a gap in the rota where she could squeeze in, so she did. While she was in there, one of the disciplinarians burst in and yelled, "What are you doing in here! This is not the time for Junior Monks!" She tried to explain. "That makes no difference. Get out! Get out!" he insisted. She left the bathhouse thinking, "My God, what an SOB." When the next bath day arrived, she looked over the schedule again and slipped in another gap further down the seniority list. But he turned up again, yelling even louder. The third time this happened, the poor woman reached the end of her rope, and in essence "gave up." No more explanations, no more appeals. Then, as she looked into his face, she realized there was no malice in him at all. "I'm sorry," she said, "but I don't know what to do." A smile spread across his face and he replied, "Don't worry, we'll figure something out." Then she knew that the point all along was to give her the opportunity to drop her self-centered concerns while face-to-face with a senior. Cutting through her opinions of what was fair, and of how the disciplinarian "should" treat her, she faced the monster of mythic proportions. She passed the test, made a friend, and in that moment stood far beyond praise and blame, self and other.

In 1986, during the events described in the Chapter titled *The Dragon's Jaws*, Gyokuko and I dropped our affiliation with the monastery where we were trained. As I mentioned earlier, issues of power and obedience to a central authority arose that in our opinion would have required turning over our personal wills in a way contrary to what we had been taught. Our center in Oregon became independent at that time. Because of those events, and even before, Gyokuko and I spent a good deal of time examining and sorting many of the things we were taught, grappling with trying to understand what in all of it was truly good, and what was dysfunctional or just not useful. Bringing some compatible psychotherapeutic processes into the mix of what we offer at our center was part of that self-examination. For me, especially, it was important to challenge myself and the way I did things over that period of a year or two. What purpose did our actions serve? Were they teaching for our students and disciples, or bad habits learned in a dysfunctional institution? There are many different styles of teaching. Are some better than others? Why do things one way and not another? It was a period of some very deep soul searching, and a time when I learned a tremendous amount from our students.

One day, all at once, came some real clarity, as if a cloud of dust had settled. I could see such wonderful perfection at the heart of the method by which we were taught. I could see its roots in the writings of many of the ancient masters. I came to realize just what I had been given, and that this is what I have to give. There are other excellent ways of teaching that are, no doubt, better suited for many people. Perhaps there are only a few for whom this way is right, and very few indeed for whom I could be a good teacher. The thing is, as I see clearly what it is I have to give, I have no need to worry about the rest. Perhaps it seems ridiculous that someone who had been a monk for seventeen years, and teaching for seven, would only then come to understand this. Come to think of it, it is ridiculous. It doesn't matter, I'm just glad I finally started getting it.

Tozan Ryokai's poem: *The Most Excellent Mirror, Samadhi*, which we recite at Morning Service, has a lot to say about the different positions of relationship that arise between master and disciple. There is a line in it which reads, "Although not made by artifice, this Truth can find expression in the words of those who teach true Zen."[17] For me, this has come to mean that I don't have to *use* praise and blame, in some deliberate way, for Rinzai's *Four Distinctions* to appear in my relationships with my students. Without trying at all, there are times my students feel affirmed by me, and times when they do not. There are times when they feel injured by me in some way, and times when they do not. It seems to happen quite naturally that we go through a progressive dance. In the beginning, I come toward them with encouragement, but later they must come toward me as their practice intensifies. Then, for us to meet on level ground, they must ultimately affirm themselves. What matters is that we each be willing to really meet the other. Then the practice and relationship develops naturally, if not always comfortably, without artifice.

Something of interest I have noticed is that as the root of the teaching becomes clearer to me, I can see the dysfunctional stuff clearly for what it is. With this comes an understanding of what I have to work on myself, especially as I stand in the position of a teacher. Training with my own ego-formations means seeing and working through all the dysfunctional elements transmitted to me from the monastery, or anywhere else, for that matter. What a wonderful practice this is. I owe endless gratitude to my teacher and all my brothers and sisters in the Sangha.

THREE PARABLES

THE OCEAN MIRROR SAMADHI

When giving meditation instruction, I often suggest a visual image. Imagine holding a bowl of water on your lap. The bowl is quite full, and you hold it in your hands, which are in the meditation mudra.* The water in the bowl is your mind, while the bowl itself is your body. Holding the bowl still is your effort in meditation. While sitting, thoughts, feelings, and bodily sensations will arise, as well as sights and sounds. They bump and jostle you as you sit with the bowl of water on your lap. If you remember to hold the bowl still, the bumps and vibrations pass through the water with barely a trace. What we usually do, though, is react with a jerk whenever a thought or feeling arises, which sloshes the water around in the bowl. The effort of meditation, just being still, allows the water to settle, to become tranquil and clear. Our habitual reactions to all these thoughts and feelings actually stir them up, so as we make this effort at stillness, the number of thoughts, memories, and sensations will begin to subside by themselves. Just letting the body settle aids the mind in becoming calm, and letting thoughts and feelings arise and pass through the mind unhindered cuts the habitual pattern of mental noise and agitation.

A commonly used method in beginning meditation practice is focusing on the breath. The breath connects the inside and outside as we inhale and exhale. It is a bridge between the conscious and the unconscious, because breathing can be either deliberate or automatic. Each inbreath is an act of acceptance as we draw the world in, and each outbreath is letting go as we release it. Breathing truly does sum up our practice. To begin, I recommend counting the breath on each

---

*A mudra is a symbolic gesture. In the meditation mudra, the hands lie in the lap, with the fingers together. The left hand is on top of the right hand, with the fingers parallel so that the left index finger is above the right index finger, and so forth. The tips of the index and little finger of the right hand just reach the bottom knuckle of their corresponding fingers on the left hand. The tips of the thumbs touch lightly, and are held above the middle finger of the left hand so that the gesture forms an oval.

outbreath, up to "ten," then starting again at "one." The reason for this is that counting upward indefinitely can become automatic, just noise in the background, as we continue our mind habits. Returning to "one" when we get to "ten" brings us back to now. Each time we come back to now, we release our habitual pattern of thinking and reacting for a moment. Coming back to now, repeatedly, each time we count ten breaths gradually breaks up the mental congestion and helps free us from the habitual noise in our heads. The habit-energy of mental patterns can accumulate, like the momentum of a heavy wheel. Each habitual thought gives the wheel another shove. After awhile, we don't even notice how much energy we devote to it. When we meditate, we simply stop giving the wheel more shoves, so in time it slows down on its own. Then one day, the mind settles and becomes clear and calm. It's a little like waking up. We suddenly notice the wall or floor we've been gazing at. All at once, we are really present. Just here and now. This is first stage samadhi, and it's a wonderful feeling. "Samadhi" means "concentration," and this stage is described as "the senses in balance." Thoughts, feelings, memories, awareness of breath, sight, sound, and all the other sensations arise and fall in a balanced way. This is very different from our usual state of clinging to thinking, or to sight, or to sensation.

Hwa Yen* Buddhists in China developed a metaphor they called "The Ocean Mirror Samadhi." It says there is a vast and wide ocean, stretching in all directions as far as the eye can see. It is round and smooth, unfathomably deep, and whole. The surface is absolutely still, so that the entire ocean, with all its colossal size and power, easily reflects like a huge mirror all the manifold phenomena of the vast cosmos. This mirror, the greatest conceivable, not only reflects the many formations of clouds, rain, and storms from all the continents, but also the innumerable stars and galaxies, with all the activities of the sentient beings found there—including miraculous scenes in the kingdoms of gods or devils. Not only the magnificent garments

---

*The Hwa Yen school of Buddhism based its teachings on the *Avatamsaka Sutra*. *Avatamsaka* means flower ornament, or garland. Hwa Yen is Chinese for Avatamsaka, while in Japanese, it is Kegon. There is a translation of this beautiful Sutra in three volumes by Thomas Cleary, published by Shambhala, 1984, 1986, and 1987.

and exquisite adornments that beautify the lustrous bodies of the angels but also the malignant glares and grimaces that make the devils' faces dreadful are all simultaneously reflected in this great "ocean mirror," without one minute detail being omitted.

Where could such an ocean-mirror exist? Beneath our superficial whims and impulses, beneath the thoughts and feelings that come and go, beneath our opinions and personal concerns, lies the One Mind. Holding that bowl of water still, we begin to open our eyes and awaken to this great "Ocean Mirror Samadhi," for that great ocean is nothing other than our own deeper mind. The monk Fa Tsang (643-712) said, "The so-called 'Ocean Mirror' symbolizes the innate Buddha Mind. When illusions are exhausted within, the mind will become serene, limpid, and infinite reflections of all phenomena will appear at one time. This may be compared to the stirring up of ocean waves when the wind blows; and their subsidence when it stops, leaving a calm and pellucid surface where all reflections may clearly be seen."[18]

INDRA'S NET [19]

In Buddhist mythology, Indra is the creator of the world. At the moment this universe came into being, Indra threw out a net that remains suspended above it. In each knot there is a small, brilliant, many-faceted jewel. The net is so arranged that the whole universe is reflected within each jewel, and we see a panorama of the universe reflected in each one. But, in addition, when you gaze into one jewel, every other individual jewel can be seen reflected there as well. This principle is called "interpenetration," and it means that the tiniest *piece* of the whole *contains* the whole within it. There is a Zen saying that a dust mote holds within itself the whole universe, and it refers to this teaching.

There is profound beauty in this, which we can experience directly. Whenever we look deeply at another person, we already hold within ourselves much of who he or she is. This is due to the "Ocean Mirror Samadhi," the deeper mind within us, that reflects clearly and accurately. It is one thing to recognize ourselves in others, but in deepest empathy we can stretch a little beyond our own limited experience to share the perspective of people who are profoundly different in background and experience from us. It is because of this deep empathy that we *can* understand not only people, but birds and wolves, killer whales and rabbits. The important thing is not to project ourselves onto them, but instead to touch a place deep within ourselves that is not dependent upon our opinions and conditioning. This is where the empathy of interpenetration is possible, and where the leap of insight about others, human or animal, comes from.

A corollary teaching to interpenetration is interdependence. It says that each thing, down to the smallest particle, is an indispensible part of a whole. One of the principles of physics is that nothing is created or "destroyed" in the sense that all created things come from preexisting energy or matter, and everything that is destroyed merely changes location or form. In the totality, nothing can be added or taken away. The Buddhist view of interdependence is that should even one particle cease to be, the whole universe would collapse.

Our own bodies demonstrate the principles of interdependence and interpenetration. The human body exists as a whole. Each organ depends upon the others, while helping to support the whole. Each organ implies the existence of the whole, so that from just one organ, we can infer a great deal about the whole being. This is the principle of interdependence. In addition, each cell carries the complete genetic blueprint for the whole being, which is, in turn, an aspect of interpenetration. But it goes even further than this. A being from a different universe could look at a human body and learn a tremendous amount about our universe. From our teeth, stomach, and digestive tract, that being could glean something about eating and the food we eat; from the lungs, "it" could infer the existence of air; from blood, the existence of the ocean; from bones, gravity can be seen; from eyes, light. So within one human form, that other being could "see" our whole universe reflected. Each of us truly is a jewel in Indra's Net.

THE MASTER, THE MONK, & THE MIRROR

In Tang Dynasty China (618-907A.D.) the Hwa Yen school used the principle of interpenetration to explain an important aspect of the master-disciple relationship. As an illustration, they developed an analogy called "The Master, the Monk, and the Mirror."[20] Imagine a master teaching Dharma to a monk in a room with a mirror. Here the mirror represents the principle of "one mind;" it is the "Ocean Mirror" that both the master and the monk gaze into in meditation. The illustration says that on the most basic level the master is simply instructing the disciple. But, at the same time, the monk is receiving instruction from the image of the master as reflected in the monk's own mind, while the master is instructing the image of the monk as reflected in his. Through this analogy, some of the implications of interpenetration can be seen. The Hwa-yen teaching goes on to say that the circle becomes complete when the master in the mind of the monk teaches the monk in the mind of the master. It takes some careful thought to grasp the significance of this, but it is right here that understanding between master and disciple is the greatest. For this to happen, both must stretch beyond the limits of personal opinion to experience the empathy of interpenetration. As a teacher, my understanding of who my students are, and of myself, grows as I see myself reflected in their eyes. I am *instructed* by this reflection. My willingness to be instructed is the "mind of the monk" in me. This is one meaning of the master in the mind of the monk teaching the monk in the mind of the master. Conversely, my students grow most quickly, and they reach toward their potential, when they see themselves through my vision of them. In this case, the monk in the mind of the·master teaches the potential master in the mind of the monk. When all possible permutations of this arrangement are working, the Dharma flows unimpeded, and master and disciple experience the Transmission of "one mind." Still, the basic arrangement of the master teaching Dharma to the disciple remains the same.

It is helpful to remember that the qualities of master and disciple are inherent in everyone and everything; but these qualities are not possessions of self. When our temple first became independent, my relationship to students practicing here began to change. After some time I realized that I was now standing in the *position* of the teacher relative to these students, whereas before, I had stood to one side. Then the teacher had been elsewhere, residing in our former parent temple. For a time I resisted this change in my life. I didn't particularly want the new responsibility, and I couldn't understand the resentment directed at me for not meeting all these new expectations. Then I realized that my actions, or lack of actions, had a much greater effect than before, regardless of my preferences, because like it or not, I was now standing in a new position—that of a teacher. It was essential that I learn to accept this fact and be fully responsible within this position. Then I realized that all my years as a disciple, entering fully into the relationship with my teacher, had indeed prepared me for this obligation. My teacher used to say that a Senior monk is one who has fully accepted being a Junior monk, and is comfortable with it. It is the same with a teacher. A teacher must become a disciple wholeheartedly, be comfortable in that position, and in his or her heart, never leave it.

Despite all my good preparation, every so often I will do something to gall one of my students. Sometimes when I mention this fact, people are surprised or shocked, which I now find very amusing. When the student takes the direct approach and tells me how he or she feels, we can usually come to an understanding. Sometimes I see that I have made a mistake; sometimes she sees the reason for my actions; sometimes we don't come to an agreement but manage to clear the air. But occasionally a student decides that it is his duty to show me that I am wrong, thinking that if I do not acquiesce to his point of view it means I am not open to receiving the teaching from him. When the student is insistent in this way, he is trying to assume the position of the teacher, and the basic arrangement of master, monk, and mirror breaks down. The master in the mind of the monk cannot teach the monk in the mind of the master if the monk loses the image of the master in his own mind. To remain in the position of disciple takes true humility, which can be very difficult. Of course, the arrangement also breaks down if the master loses the image of the monk, and this takes humility, too. It is this humility that keeps the line of Transmission open throughout time, all the way back to Shakyamuni Buddha. It is paradoxical, perhaps, that the monk grows into the role of master by not moving from the position of disciple at all. It is through the experience of "one mind," the empathy of interpenetration with the master, that the disciple comes to know deep within himself that there never was any difference between them. At such a time, the roles are not so much reversed as completed. Yet even then, neither one moves from the original position of master and disciple.

Perhaps all this sounds wildly improbable, beyond ordinary daily experience. In a way, it is. But it is only because we usually fail to see the profound significance in ordinary daily experience that the empathy of interpenetration seems so extraordinary. What is most unusual about a master-disciple relationship (that is working the way it should) is the willingness each has to look deeply at the other and to see the Buddha manifesting there. Yet this relationship remains "ordinary" because there is nothing supernatural in it. Master and disciple remain normal human beings, doing rather ordinary everyday things. For the mutual recognition of Buddhahood to take place, both of these ordinary people must learn and grow. It falls to the student, however, to stretch the most to "catch the lord" within the teacher, while it falls to the teacher to make the Dharma accessible to the student at whatever level he or she may be.

There are good lessons for us here regarding many of our relationships in daily life. As friends, enemies, spouses, parents, children, bosses, and employees, in all these relationships, we can experience the empathy of interdependence and interpenetration. To me this is deeply significant, because many Americans suffer from a kind of identity crisis due to the loss of a clear sense of relationship to people and things around them. Meanwhile, many others feel deeply isolated, with no sense of community. I believe this is directly related to the great reluctance so many of us have to fully accepting our roles of relationship whenever they seem confining, or not as we would want them to be. This is certainly the first big stumbling block a student must overcome in the master-disciple relationship, just as it was for me in recognizing my new role as a teacher. It arises from a belief that there is a permanent "self" that is defined by the relationship. Some new disciples reject the confinement of discipleship and struggle against the very thing that offers the teaching they seek. On the other hand, some become attached to it, finding comfort in the role of "disciple," once they have learned to play it. Not moving from the position of disciple in relationship to a teacher doesn't mean always taking on a deferential demeanor. It is much more open-ended than that. Just learning a mode of behavior is taking a few beginning steps on the path, then getting stuck. Nonetheless, the freedom of Zen can be touched in any circumstance, even one of real confinement. A man or woman in prison cannot know freedom of mind and heart without first acknowledging and accepting their relationship to walls and jailers; that is, the very fact of their bodily confinement. But indeed there are prisoners who find that deeper freedom. Perhaps daily life is more like a prison than we want to acknowledge. We are trapped in human bodies, and we cannot escape the basic fact of being who we are in this life. Nor can we escape the times in which we live nor our relationships to our fellows.

Interpenetration teaches us that, as a jewel in Indra's net, we hold within ourselves the whole universe. But we cannot know this unless we accept the fact of being exactly where we are in this net. In one sense, relationships are strangely eternal. Our parents will always be our parents, and our children will remain our children, although the nature of these relationships changes. Even after a divorce, the fact of the marriage cannot be erased. That two people had been so intimately linked will continue to affect them as they go their separate ways. So I'm not saying we are all fixed in static relationships, eternal and unchanging. But at each moment important elements of relationship are present. We would do well to consider them deeply, for these elements of relationship are facets in the jewels of Indra's Net that beckon us to see into the truth of One Mind.

The teaching of interdependence adds that the whole of Indra's Net depends upon each knot. Untie one knot, and the net would unravel. We all need each other in just this way. The fact of the matter is, we can only understand ourselves through relationship, and it is only through relationship that we can understand others. Friends, enemies, spouses, parents, children, bosses, and employees, all stand in relationship to each other in much the same way as the master, the monk, and mirror. There is so much we can learn from each other. Accepting ourselves, accepting those around us, accepting our relationships to them, we can understand how we hold within ourselves everything we see in others. We can understand how much of who we are is in *response* to others. Seeing this clearly leads to real freedom. We can learn not to be trapped by old patterns, blindly responding to circumstance. When one enemy sees herself in the eyes of the other, she has touched the empathy of interpenetration. The result will be greater insight into herself, the nature of the relationship, and her enemy. Without moving an inch, the relationship will be transformed for both of them. In everyday life, we stand in relationship to everyone and everything around us. We are constantly gazing into the mirror of "one mind" that binds us together as part of Indra's net.

APPENDIX

Notes On Zazen Practice

During my years of teaching meditation and answering questions from those newly engaged in zazen practice, I have noticed several questions that are quite common, coming not only from beginners, but also from people who have been practicing for some time. I would like to share these questions and some answers in the hope that it may be of benefit.

Every so often someone will tell me that he has been sitting for several years but can only manage full lotus for a short time, and that even half-lotus becomes too much to bear after thirty or forty minutes. He will go on to describe pitched battles with ego as the time to sit approaches in which every excuse imaginable not to sit presents itself. Then he may ask for some advice on overcoming the physical and mental resistance he is experiencing. Here we have an excellent example of someone pushing much too hard just to conform to an ideal of what Zen practice should be. Even if you are sitting on a bench or a chair, if this description sounds very much like you, please be more gentle with yourself. Turning the flow of compassion within begins with treating your body with respect and care. It is neither necessary nor wise to strain to maintain any posture, and signs that you are pushing too hard should not be ignored. We have been given an aversion to pain for a very good reason. If the body is sending signals that something is wrong, we set body and mind against each other when we grit our teeth in stubborn refusal to give in to it. Of course, it is good to make an effort to improve our physical ability to sit, but zazen should never become an endurance test. If we approach zazen with gentle determination and a bright mind, we will look forward to sitting with eagerness. It is really terrible, and completely unnecessary, to face meditation with dread. Too much rigidity in practice makes it joyless, and when it is, people either drift off to other things or become joyless themselves. Dogen says we should sit in a way that is naturally joyful,[1] and so it can be. When it is, zazen remains a practice that will enrich us all the years of our lives. I always recommend sitting for as long as it is comfortable in a given posture, then making the effort to sit for a little while longer. After that, change to another position, or do walking meditation for a few minutes, then resume sitting. Meditation done well for five or ten minutes is far superior to hours of self-torture, so please don't strain to achieve an ideal form, and please don't be in a hurry to progress physically, or you'll defeat the deeper purpose of zazen. The posture should be so still, centered, and comfortable that the mind is alert and completely relaxed.

I remember how surprised I was to discover that the lotus postures are recommended precisely for their comfort, and also because the postures are a physical expression of what we are trying to achieve in meditation. Sitting in full- or half-lotus holds your hips in a position that makes your back naturally erect, because it places your shoulders directly over your hips. This forms a vertical axis right through your upper torso, so that you feel physically centered. This is also a posture of great awareness, just like when you sit on the edge of your chair at the climax of a movie. In zazen this principle is applied in reverse; by holding ourselves erect, we very easily remain alert. Further advantages include the triangular formation made when we sit crosslegged, which gives great lateral stability to the posture, and the way the position of the hips gives stability front to back. This stability helps us to remain extremely still without conscious effort to hold ourselves upright. Since we are not reclining against any surface, our circulation is not impeded and there is no need to fidget. In this attitude of still, alert, centered comfort we find the essence of meditation to which tortured endurance bears no resemblance. So, although there is good reason to want to develop the ability to use the cross-egged postures well, straining to do so defeats their purpose and discourages meditation practice. It is better to sit comfortably and regularly on a chair or kneeling (which lack only the lateral stability of crosslegged postures) and gradually work into Burmese or one of the lotus positions when and if it feels right.

The question of how hard to push in meditation also comes up with regard to the length of time we spend doing it, regardless of posture. People these days are very busy, and it seems as though there are more demands on our time than there are hours in a day. It is bad enough when the mind wanders and we get restless and start to fidget, but it is worse when we feel the call of half-a-dozen things demanding our attention. You can almost hear the clock ticking in someone's head when that happens. The problem arises partly because we try to separate the time for meditation from everything else we do. There are many times that this is actually very good to do, but not when it creates a conflict in our own minds about what we should be doing. Just as trying to conform to an ideal posture can set body and mind at odds, so can trying to conform to a set time of day or duration of time for meditation practice. If you don't decide ahead of time that you are going to sit for twenty or thirty minutes, you can bypass the issue of "budgeting time." If this has been a problem for you, try sitting without any predetermined length of time in mind. Decide that you are only going to sit for as long as it feels good to do so. It is so much easier to begin the practice when you can't fail to meet your "quota." As you relax more deeply into sitting, time goes by very easily. Sometimes you will sit for just five or ten minutes, but you will have done so wholeheartedly. At other times, time will slip by and you will realize that for that day, the twenty or thirty minutes was very well spent. Some days you may find that the urgency of other demands is such that you really should be doing something else. So realizing that, off you go. What I am describing here is a way of letting the deeper mind set your meditation timer for you. It is also a way of harmonizing your practice with all the other things you need to be doing in your life, rather than pitting practice against everything else. This is why very busy people find coming to the Zendo here at the Center all the more important. Once here, a block of time has been committed to the practice. The bells and gongs are in the hands of the Time Keeper, and the schedule for sittings and services are set for the benefit of all attending. Sharing practice with other people makes the time spent a mutual contract between all those there, so it becomes something shared. Rather than just taking time for ourselves, we are also giving it to others, and this makes the practice easier to do.

When to sit can be as difficult to work out as how long to sit. Once again, for busy people with many demands on their time, flexibility within a firm commitment is very important. We once worked with a professional couple with two small children. They were a classic example of very heavily committed people, with unending pulls on their time. At one point, they realized they could tie their evening zazen schedule to their children's bedtime. They would sit as soon as both children were asleep, a time of profound quiet, I was assured. They made a promise to each other to do this for a specific period of time, say three months, except when they had guests, or when their children fell asleep after a specified cut-off point, in which case they let it go for the evening. This way they were committed to regular practice but did not set that practice against the other things they needed to do.

We have made a commitment at the Zen Center to adapt Zen practice to the needs of lay people. We think of the Center as being similar to the Zendo in a Zen monastery. Only the Junior monks have the luxury of living in the Zendo, and of following a daily schedule based entirely on the rhythm of the meditation hall. The Senior monks live in quarters around the hall and look after the various departments necessary for the running of the temple. I know from experience that the demands on Senior monks can mean that there are times when they don't set foot in the Zendo for weeks. I had to take my meditation in my room when I could get it, just like busy laymen. The disadvantage of lay practice is not having the opportunity to spend several years in training as a Junior monk, and of course laypeople are more at the whim of circumstance than a Senior monk. But for all other intents and purposes, lay practice is very much the same as that of Senior monks. Both must work to make their lives an expression of Zen practice, without relying on the support of monastic forms. The Zen Center is here to help people do that.

Another question that often arises has to do with how to handle the many thoughts, emotions, memories, and such that can be so distracting during meditation. I have found that people can vary quite a bit in the types of things that arise to distract them. One person may be appalled to discover the first time she sits that her thoughts rampage through her mind like a runaway train. Another may find sitting fairly easy and pleasant at first, but a little later discover that whatever emotion is uppermost in his life at that time becomes intensified and almost unbearable during meditation.

Let us first consider the case of runaway thoughts. I have heard descriptions of monumental battles people get into when trying to control their thoughts. While we should not let ourselves be carried away by distracting thoughts, sometimes called Monkey Mind, we do better to accept them gently, compassionately, and wholeheartedly. We should start by embracing our own tendency towards Monkey Mind patiently, as one would the prattlings of a small child. There is nothing wrong with having an active mind, only in making it the center of your being. The stillness of meditation lies beneath the chattering of the thinking mind, not beyond and separate from it. Have you ever been sitting in meditation and suddenly realized that you have been a hundred miles away for the last 20 minutes? "Oh, no! Now I have to start over," you may think. Or perhaps you will bear down extra hard to make up for lost time. But the moment you realize that you have drifted off somewhere, you are, right at that moment of recognition, meditating perfectly. What could be added to this awareness? By gently accepting Monkey Mind, it is conquered, and the habitual prattling of thoughts we have grown so accustomed to will gently subside by itself.

People have told me that when distracting thoughts seem especially persistent, they will sometimes break the train of thought by a process something like mentally "blinking." I think it can be good to do this occasionally if it is done to help grab the will; but be extremely careful of making a practice of repressing thoughts. At one time in my own training, I became very good at repressing thought altogether, thinking that "emptying" my mind had something to do with the "emptiness" mentioned in the Sutras. Then one day during a meal I suddenly lost the right side of my vision. Everything to the right of a place extending directly out from my nose simply vanished. My vision gradually returned, but it was these very disturbing several minutes that brought a clear message to relax my practice.

My feeling is that when distracting thoughts persist, one of the best ways to handle them is to count your breath. This is done by counting each breath as you exhale, breathing slowly and deeply, but naturally. When you get to ten, start again at one. It helps to know there is a difference between awareness, or consciousness, and thought. By being aware of your breathing, you become aware that your consciousness goes far deeper than the thinking process. As you focus awareness on the still depths beneath thought, the thoughts will subside by themselves, simply because you stop investing energy in them. As you do this, you are learning to "live" in a place deeper than your own head. In time, you will feel a "settling" of body and mind, a relaxation into meditation. As this settling continues, it can help to stop counting your breath and simply follow it; that is, to watch each breath come in and go out without counting. As the relaxation becomes complete, you can let go of following the breath and concentrate on "just sitting." From here, meditation can take many forms, some extraordinarily deep, some ecstatic, some less deep but very meaningful. It is important not to expect anything but to simply prepare yourself for whatever experience is to be given. After all, it is a gift, and not something that can be achieved or taken by force.

Just as it is with distracting thoughts, so it is with any other problem that arises during meditation, whether it is intense emotion, feelings of inadequacy, resistance to the teaching, or daydreaming. Since meditation is a process of getting beyond self, all the ways in which we cling to self stand out in sharp relief as we progress. It can help to realize that increased awareness of our own attachments is a sign of progress if we are willing to learn from it. But always it is through gentle acceptance of our limitations that we deepen our awareness of the Buddha Nature. The very thing within ourselves that recognizes and accepts these limitations *is* our own deeper mind, our own Buddha Nature, so there is nothing else to be done.

Over the centuries, Buddhist sages have observed themselves from the perspective of meditation. Buddhist teachings have arisen from this collective observation, and they have much to offer that can help us understand our own experiences. One such teaching is that a sentient being is composed of five skandhas, or aggregates, which are arranged in successive layers. They are: *form*, which is the physical body; the next layer down is *sensation*, or feelings, both physical and emotional; then comes *thought*, which is the mental level of a being; next is *activity*, which refers to drive, or volition; and finally there is *consciousness* itself. Buddhist teaching on the skandhas also says that these five aggregates of being are subject to change and so have no permanent *separate* self-nature. They are therefore, "sunya," or empty. But this emptiness also means that they are fundamentally pure in that they are neither separate from, nor do they in any way impede, the Buddha Nature.

From this teaching, I have come to view the five skandhas as the objects of five delusions of self. When we grasp after, or become attached to one of them, we are giving substance to an illusory sense of self. The first is the belief that "I am my body." Excessive concern for health or beauty or body building are examples of this. The second is "I am my feelings." The Romantic Age epitomizes this, and some schools of pop psychology seem to indulge in this also. Third is "I am my thoughts." Descartes formulated the classic expression of this when he stated "I think, therefore I am." This one seems to be the most pervasive in the West as we place so much importance on our own opinions. Number four comes out as "I am what I do." This is very common among highly motivated, career-oriented people. "I am a doctor, lawyer, nurse, artist, mother, father, sage." It can also be formulated, "I am my drive to become ... wealthy, successful, famous." And finally, the most subtle and dangerous of all, "I am my consciousness." It is here that the mistake is made of turning the religious quest into a possession of self.

The practice of meditation is learning to "live" in the stillness beneath all change, which is the true center, or the point at which "we" and "Cosmic Buddha" intersect. To do this is to express Buddha Nature. The case of the woman who finds her thoughts running away with her during sitting is a case of "living in her head." This is the tendency that leads to the delusion, "I am my thoughts." In many ways this problem is easy to get a handle on, because in meditation at least, it is easy to recognize that thoughts are getting in the way. The second case, that of having emotions linger and intensify while sitting, is an example of living in the realm of sensation. The pull to identify with our feelings is very strong. Since people are a thorough mixture of all five skandhas, attachment to each will come up at one point or another. But these two, thought and sensation, come up first and are the most common. Still, the others will come up in time. The clue to how to handle these distracting attachments is found in the teaching that the skandhas are absolutely pure and not separate from the Buddha Nature in any way. The first thing we are taught when starting to sit is "do not try to think," "do not try not to think," and simply to let things come and go without becoming involved in them. Just how wise and deep this teaching is becomes clear when we realize that it applies to every one of the five delusions of self, just as it does to the first distracting thoughts that obscure meditation.

Another question I hear now and then has to do with glimpses of an exquisite state of mind, or of realizations that occur during meditation. But as soon as this tantalizing state arises and is recognized, it suddenly vanishes and seems to recede further than ever. What is usually happening in cases like this is that the desire to know this exquisiteness leads to trying to catch it with the mind, or to cling to the sensation of it. Like water in the hand, it vanishes as soon as the fingers close around it. Experiences like these are to consciousness as sights are to the eye and sounds to the ear. They are not a quality of consciousness itself. They arise and fall in their own time and cannot be caught and held. It does no good to worry about whether they will come or not, nor can we try to chase them. We can only concentrate on our "just sitting," and on meditation in daily life. When these experiences come, let them come; and when they go, let them go: just like thoughts in zazen. Our part in this is the "just sitting." The Buddha Mind will manifest naturally, but it will not respond to our demands.

For many years I wondered why it was that consciousness should be included in the five skandhas that are subject to change and therefore empty. Consciousness is our very deepest awareness, but it does change over time. It is through consciousness that we first glimpse and then come to know the Buddha; but it is by "just sitting" that we allow this door to open. We cannot cling to these experiences any more than we can cling to our first taste of fresh spring water. The more we experience and the more we learn, the greater the danger becomes of clinging to these things as a possession of self. When this happens, our own experiences become "the Buddha that gets in the way." They become just another delusion of self. Then we have to learn to get beyond them if we want to continue on the spiritual path. Like the other skandhas, however, consciousness is pure and fundamentally part of the Buddha Nature. When we just sit and let go of our clinging to consciousness, the mind of meditation arises again and new experiences are possible. What is more, our past experiences are again seen as valuable Dharma instead of as possessions of self. It is a source of endless wonder to me that the meditation practice we learn in the very beginning, just letting things come and go without clinging, is all we really need all along the entire length of the path of training. It is just as Dogen says in "Fukanzazengi": "That which we call zazen is not a way of developing concentration. It is simply the comfortable way. It is practice which measures your satori to the fullest, and is in fact satori itself."*

---

*"Fukanzazengi" means "recommendations for doing zazen." This quote is from a translation by Francis Dojun Cook, in *How To Raise An Ox*, Center Publications, Los Angeles, 1978, p.97.

NOTES

THE MIND THAT SEEKS THE WAY

[1] Title page inscription in *The Great Natural Way*, by Ven. Honzen Seki, 1976, American Buddhist Academy, New York.

[2] "In Memoriam, A.H.H." Canto 96, St. 3. Written for Arthur Henry Hallam in 1850.

[3] The "Mahayana Shraddhotpada Shastra," or "Awakening of Faith in the Mahayana," is a Sanskrit text that was very influential in Chinese Buddhism. For a translation, see *A Buddhist Bible*, edited by Dwight Goddard, E.P. Dutton, 1966, pp. 357-404.

[4] Whereas I have been unable to find a source for the first quote, the second can be found in *More Quotable Chesterton*, ed. Marlin, Rabatin, and Swan, 1988, Ignatius Press, San Francisco. It comes from the American edition of The Illustrated London News, June 20th, 1914.

[5] For his arguments on this, see the "Introductory Remarks on the Importance of Orthodoxy" pp. 11-24, and the "Concluding Remarks on the Importance of Orthodoxy" pp. 285-305 in *Heretics*, John Lane Company, New York & London, 1914.

[6] See "Guidelines for Studying the Way," in *Moon In A Dewdrop*, ed. by Kazuaki Tanahashi, North Point Press, San Francisco, 1985, pp. 31-33; or "Gyakudoyojinshu" in *Selling Water By The River*, Jiyu Kennett, Pantheon, 1972, pp. 103-105.

[7] See "Fukanzazengi," or "General Recommendations for Doing Zazen" in *How To Raise An Ox*, Francis Dojun Cook, Center Publication, Los Angeles, CA, 1978, p. 95.

IN EVERYDAY LIFE

[1] Although I remember my teacher reading this story and commenting on it, I have been unable to find any reference to it. I cannot say for sure that it is actually from the Zen tradition.

[2] See *The Outsider*, Colin Wilson, Readers Union, London, 1957.

[3] See "Shushogi," in *Soto Shu Sutras*, various translators, Soto Shu Shumucho, Tokyo, Japan, 1984, pages 33 & 34.

[4] *Zen Flesh, Zen Bones*; Paul Reps, Anchor Books (no date) p.21.

[5] Case 43 of the Mumonkan, or *Gateless Gate*, as it appears in Reps, op cit, p.124.

[6] See the glossary entry in *Selling Water By The River*, Jiyu Kennett, Pantheon, New York, 1972, p. 316.

[7] "See The Time-Being," *Uji* in *Moon In A Dewdrop*, edited by Kazuaki Tanahashi, North Point Press, San Francisco, 1985, p. 78.

[8] Information on this is in the Transmission Papers given to Soto priests, and is not readily available.

[9] Tanahashi, op cit, p. 70. This is in Dogen's "Genjokoan," which has been translated and made available in a number of different works.

FACING THE DRAGON

[1] This verse by Setcho Juken (Xuedou Zhongxian, 980-1052) was quoted by Dogen in his "Tenzo-kyokan," or "Instructions to the Chief Cook." There are many translations, varying considerably. See *Refining Your Life*, Kosho Uchiyama (Thomas Wright, translator), Weatherhill, Tokyo, 1987, p.12. Also, Tanahashi, op. cit., p. 60. And Kennett, op. cit., p. 153.

[2] As found in *Zen Poetry*, edited and translated by Lucien Stryk and Takashi Ikemoto, Penguin Books, 1981, p. 67.

[3] Dogen's *Uji* (Existence, Time) as translated by Kennett, op. cit., p. 141.

[4] *Shushogi* is a compilation of Dogen's writings done by the Soto Zen Sect as a primer of Zen teaching. See *Selling Water By The River*, trans. by Roshi Jiyu-Kennett, Pantheon, NY, 1972, p. 135. Also, *Soto Shu Sutras*, various translators, no editor listed, Soto Shu Shumucho, Tokyo, p. 35.

[5] See Tanahashi, op cit, pp. 74-75; or Kennett, op cit, pp. 136-137.

[6] Blue Cliff Records, Case 53. See *The Blue Cliff Records*, R.D.M. Shaw d.d., Michael Joseph, London, 1961, p.176.

[7] According to Pastor Fred Riess, Archivist for the Northwest District Office of the Lutheran church, Missouri Synod, stories like this one, in which there is *physical* interaction between Martin Luther and the Devil, are common and often repeated. There is no basis for any of them in Luther's writings, however.

[8] *Zen: Poems, Prayers, Sermons, Anecdotes, Interviews;* ed. & trans. by Lucien Stryk and Takashi Ikemoto, Doubleday Anchor, Garden City, NY, pp. 115-116. This is a slightly edited version of that story.

[9] Zen Flesh, Zen Bones, Compiled by Paul Reps, Doubleday Anchor, Garden City NY, no date, p. 41.

[10] For a discussion of single enlightenment, see pp 55-57.

[11] See Shushogi, Soto Shu Shumucho, op cit, p. 34. Also, Kennett, op cit, p. 134.

[12] See Shoji in Tanahashi, op cit, p. 75; or Shoji in Kennett, op cit, p. 136.

[13] The Penguin Book of Zen Poetry, Lucien Stryk and Takashi Ikemoto, Penguin Books, NY, 1981, p. 77.

[14] Mockingbird Books, Covington, Georgia, 1975.

[15] "Shushogi" in Soto Shu Sutras, op cit, p. 29; also Shushogi in Kennett, op cit, p. 129.

[16] Lin Chi (Rinzai, a.d. 866) said that when his disciples brought him their understanding, sometimes he would: snatch away the person, but save the object (their expression); snatch away the object, but save the person; snatch away both person and object; snatch away neither. For a discussion of this, see The Practice of Zen, Garma C.C. Chang, Perennial Library, 1959, pp. 175-176.

[17] Soto Shu Sutras, Hokklyozanmai, op. cit., p. 17.

[18] This quote may be found in The Buddhist Teaching of Totality, The Philosophy of Hwa Yen Buddhism, by Garma C.C. Chang, Pennsylvania State University Press, 1974, p. 125. I am also indebted to Chang for his description of the ocean mirror, from which I borrowed heavily.

[19] For a discussion of this analogy, see ibid, p. 165-166.

[20] For a discussion of this analogy, see ibid, p. 126.

APPENDIX

[1] See "Bendowa" in Kennet. op cit., p. 115; or Shobogenzo, Vol. I, Kosen Nishayama and John Stevens, Daihokkaikaku, Tokyo, 1975, p. 147.